Published by *Access Press*
P.O. Box 132, Northbridge, Western Australia 6865

Copyright © John Harper-Nelson, 1996

This book is copyright. Apart from any fair dealing for the purpose of private study, research, criticism or review, as permitted under the Copyright Act, no part may be reproduced by any process without written permission. Enquiries should be made to the publisher.

Typesetting, layout and design by *Access Press*

National Library of Australia
Cataloguing in Publication data
Oxford at War
ISBN 0 949795 92 5

Distributed in Australia and Overseas by the Publisher.

Oxford at War

An Undergraduate Memoir
John Harper-Nelson 1940–42

This is an
ACCESS PRESS
Publication

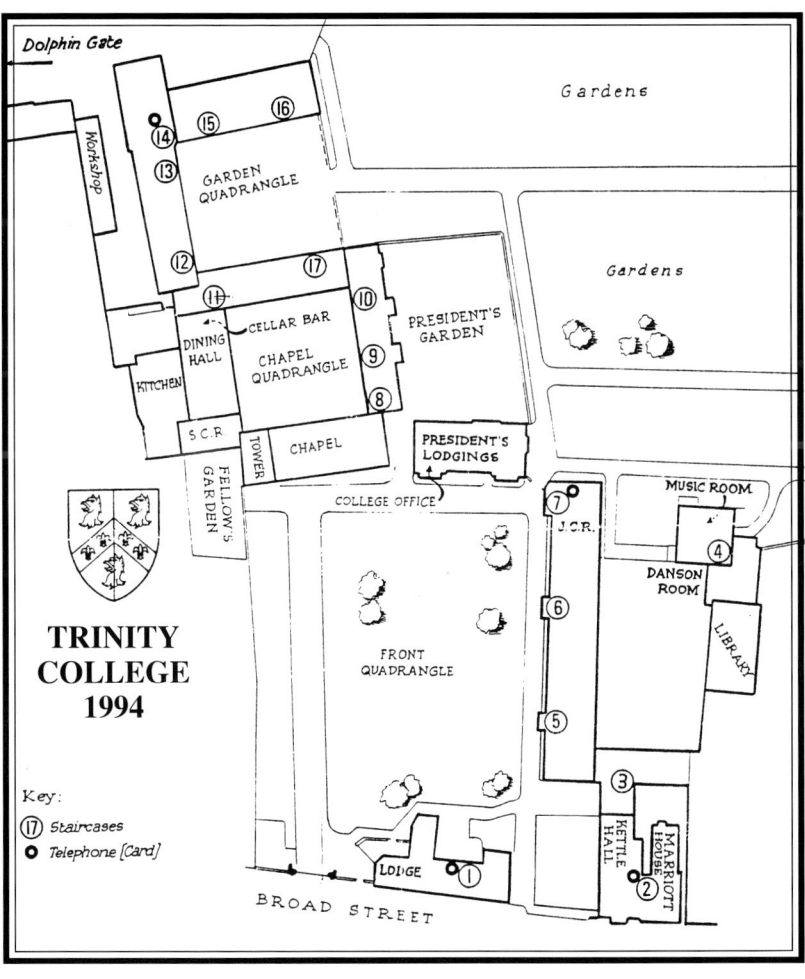

Trinity College undergraduates 1941.

DEDICATION
To David, Vernon, Paddy and all those
who made being at Oxford such fun
but didn't live to enjoy the memories.

FOREWORD

On a visit to Oxford in the 1980's I was amazed to find that there were few records of life in my College or, indeed, the University in general during the war years 1940 to 1942.

I had vivid memories of the time I spent there from Michaelmas 1940 to the end of Hilary 1942. Five terms in all, but what a crowded time it was.

Unfortunately I have never managed to keep a diary so that when I came to write my memories down I had to rely on frequent prompting from the College archivists Bryan Ward-Perkins and, especially, Clare Hopkins as to which term certain events took place. Permission to quote from James Agate's "Ego 5" was obtained from Larousse-Harrap. Glynne Wickham kindly provided me with photographs of himself and Nevill Coghill.

I have quoted extensively from the Cherwell magazine because it largely represented undergraduate attitudes of the time. For this and other extracts from Oxford papers of the period I am grateful to Julie-Ann Lambert and the staff of the John Johnson collection and room 132 at the Bodleian library. Where I have failed to locate an author or photographer for acknowledgement, I beg their forgiveness.

But this is a personal reminiscence. I have not attempted to write a history of the period. There is no grand design. This is simply what happened to me and what I did, who I met, who my friends were and how we behaved. In this way I have tried to give a fair impression of what life was like in Trinity particularly and Oxford generally all those years ago. In doing so I have confined myself to events in which I was personally involved. No doubt lots of other things were taking place of far greater import but I wasn't there and didn't see them. In fact, on looking back, I am rather ashamed at how trivial my activities seem to have been, but perhaps there is the excuse that in the midst of the desperate seriousness of life around us, we chose to be defiantly light hearted.

I particularly want to dedicate this book to the memory of those dear friends who helped to make being at Trinity such fun but who never lived to enjoy the memories. To them and all those others, I offer this memorial with love.

John Harper Nelson.

CHAPTER ONE

It was a relief to get to Oxford for the Michaelmas term 1940.

From May 6th, when the Local Defence Volunteers had been formed, I had been on various forms of duty. First of all it had been sporadic periods of guard duty round about Victoria Station during the so-called "nuisance raids" throughout the Summer, but from September 1st it had been almost continuous duty during the height of the "Blitz" so that the retreat into the tranquility of Trinity in October seemed like a transition from war to peace.

Getting to Oxford from London had been an exercise in wartime logistics. Luggage was still of the seaborne kind; cabin trunk, heavy leather suitcase, my old wooden school tuck box, were piled into the taxi beside the driver. I had chosen an early train so that my sister Margaret, who insisted on seeing me off, could get back to Dolphin Square before the sirens went.

Paddington had been bombed. I had seen it happen only a few days earlier. Looking out from the window of our sixth floor flat in Rodney House after the All Clear had sounded, I had seen a single plane flying low just above the barrage balloons heading East. It never occurred to me that it might be an enemy plane until I saw the bombs fall. Four tiny lozenges dropped from the plane's belly like a bird relieving itself, then the distant plumes of smoke showed where they had hit. It was Paddington Station during the rush hour that always followed the All Clear.

It was an impersonal observation, just as seeing the fires flare up in the docklands or the wreck of a Heinkel balanced on top of Walkers the jewellers outside Victoria Station was impersonal. I knew that they indicated death and destruction, pain and misery, but after the initial anger that such things could happen it was surprising how quickly the mind became deadened to anything but the detached registration of the facts. Now, on the way to Oxford, I could see the wreckage.

"Sorry, Sir, this is as close as I can get," the taxi driver had said as he deposited us in the street. But there was a porter to take the luggage and pilot me to the train. It was early afternoon. Clusters of people stood awkwardly round each open door making heavy conversation while they hoped that the whistle would blow.

"Don't stay I'll be fine."

"Bye-bye darling, look after yourself. Don't forget to write", and my sister had gone, heading for the comparative safety of the Underground. My porter was hovering at the carriage door.

"Got you a corner seat, Sir. Thank you, Sir," not looking at his tip. A whistle blew and the engine let loose an ear splitting burst of high-pressure steam. Doors slammed and late arrivals struggled on board. I squeezed into my seat as the train gave a lurch and then cautiously eased its way past piles of fallen masonry and a wrecked carriage. A gang of railway workers stood aside as the train passed, pausing impassively from their work of replacing a section of the line that had been picked up, crumpled and tossed aside like a piece of discarded knitting. It was a blurred image anyway because the window was criss-crossed with strips of sticky tape to stop it shattering from bomb blast.

The people in the train sat wedged together gazing into space or pretending to read. They were standing shoulder to shoulder in the corridor and a couple of aircraftsmen were standing swaying in the middle of the compartment astride their kit bags. It wasn't an easy place to have tried to hold a private conversation.

Once beyond Ealing Broadway the train seemed to sense open fields and freedom and speeded up. It stopped at Slough, Reading and Didcot, familiar country to me because this was the Cheltenham line where, before the war, the Cheltenham

Flyer had been the world's fastest train, hammering along at over a hundred miles an hour between Swindon and Ealing. Now, after a long brooding halt at Didcot, the train puffed off along the Oxford line.

Oxford was one of those places like Cheltenham where they hadn't approved of the railway in the early days so that the line comes in almost surreptitiously on the edge of town, past Victorian red brick, with barely a glimpse of a dreaming spire unless you know where to look.

It was not my first visit. During the Summer I had spent three days taking a college entrance exam after intensive coaching at a crammer I had attended in Holland Park. My tutor, John Hyde, was disappointed that I did not succeed as he had been sure that his old college, Balliol, would welcome me. Balliol did not and it was some time later that I realised that their suggestion that I should try Trinity was probably a subversive donnish joke.

Trinity, fortunately, relied on an interview to establish that one went to the right sort of school, had a reasonable command of the King's English and seemed to be the sort of person who would fit happily into the confines of a small and rather exclusive college. My failure to meet the scholastic demands of the college on the other side of the wall was one of the happier accidents of my generally fortunate life.

It was Michaelmas Term. Drizzling rain and rugby goal-posts.

I queued in the rain and got a taxi, clutching my suitcase and being assured that my luggage in the Guard's van would be duly delivered to the college by lorry.

Unlike most of the colleges which have a fortress-like appearance, guarded by heavy gates flanked by barred windows from which it wouldn't be surprising to be greeted by a shower of arrows, Trinity presents an open and smiling face. The porter's lodge is tucked away demurely beside the great iron gates that open onto an ornamental orchard backed by a neat chapel.

I paid off the taxi with a generous shilling tip and the college porter checked the roll.

"Staircase eleven, room thirteen, Chapel quad, Sir. The

College servants will see to your luggage when it comes and there's some mail for you, Sir, on the board there."

I found my two letters thrust into the cross gartered mail board and put them in my pocket to read in the quietness of my room where-ever that was. Suddenly I felt like a new boy at school. I thought of my parents in India and wished they could see me now. Then I thought of my sister in London and wondered how the night would be there. Embarrassed I realised that tears had welled up in my eyes. I seized my suitcase and headed for the Chapel.

An archway under the Chapel tower led into a small neat quad and in the far left hand corner I found Staircase Eleven. The steep wooden stairs took me to a landing where I paused for breath.

"Can I help you, Sir?"

A stocky middle-aged man in a white jacket was coming down the next flight.

"I'm North, Sir, This is my staircase so I expect that I'll be looking after you for a few terms. Number thirteen is up here."

He led the way to a door on the left of a short corridor which opened into a sombre sitting room. There was a threadbare carpet, brown furniture, brownish wall paper, brownish curtains backed by the black ones required for the black-out. Two small windows looked out onto the Chapel quad. From this room another door led into the bedroom. A faded rug lay beside the iron bedstead. There was a brown wardrobe, a wash stand with a hole in the top to hold the china basin in which there stood a ewer full of water. Beside the bed there was a brown bentwood chair and on the other side a bedside cupboard in which there nestled a china po like a giant tea-cup. Under the wash-stand there was a large enamel slop bucket. There wasn't time to explore further because North was talking.

"Breakfast is from eight to eight-fortyfive, Sir, and most Gentlemen like to be called about seven fifteen. I bring you a cup of tea and hot water for shaving. There's a scuttle of coal beside the fireplace in the sitting room if you feel cold in the evening but there's only one scuttle a day allowed with the war on." He made it sound as if someone had left the war on just to

Unlike most of the colleges, Trinity presents a smiling face.

be awkward. "And this door here," he indicated a large plain wooden door that lay back against the corridor wall, "this is your oak. If you want to be private you can close this and no-one can get in because there's only this bolt on the inside. Once you've sported your oak, Sir, the only way anyone can contact you is by popping a note through this slit here." He demonstrated the impregnability of the oak and continued his recital.

"I'll make up your bed as soon as your luggage is brought up and the bathrooms and lavatories are out the back down the stairs through the arch past the Hall and keep going till you get to the bath-house. It's a tidy walk on a cold morning. Have you got a torch?"

"In my suitcase."

"You'll need a torch. It gets as black as pitch round the college buildings at night when there's no moon. Now I'll leave you to sort yourself out."

"Thank you Mr North."

"Just North, Sir. Thank you, Sir, I hope you'll be comfortable."

As he bustled off I could hear other arrivals struggling up the stairs no doubt to be greeted by North's standard recital.

College regulations had decreed that I arrive equipped with two pairs of sheets, two pillow cases, two dusters, two toilet covers whatever they might be, two glass cloths, and three bath and three hand towels. I opened my suitcase and took out my camel hair dressing gown and flannel pyjamas and laid them on the bed to show that I was ready to occupy it in due course. Then I arranged my shaving kit neatly on the washstand and burrowed under assorted pullovers and underwear for my torch.

As I went down stairs I looked at the names on the board at the foot of the staircase and wondered what they were all like and hoped they would be friendly. J. Evans, E.M. Lock, V. St John, E. Straghan, R. Drury, D. Davies, D. Marsh, myself, P. Engelbach, S. Partridge. Staircase eleven, Michaelmas 1940.

My father, who had taken his medical degree in Edinburgh, had told me that the best way to make friends was to join things. It wasn't a problem for a freshman at Oxford. The problem was trying not to join. I had hardly had time to arrange my room before the stream of visitors started. Rugby, hockey, cricket, rowing, squash, swimming, athletics, religious denominations, debating. choirs, orchestras, chamber music, poetry, politics, drama and dance all had their eager protagonists knocking at the door selling their wares.

The college captain of rugby was a chap called Colson, glowing with health and determination, He was also, I believe, the secretary of the University Rugby Club - a blue no less.

It is always assumed that if you went to a school that had a reputation for excellence in any sport, you were automatically good at it. Cheltenham College was known as a rugby school but I had never made it into the first XV except as cannon fodder to replace more valuable but vulnerable players in confrontations with tough uncompromising teams like Cheltenham Town where burly artisans were only too keen to trample those uppity schoolboys into the mud. The top players were reserved for the prestigious and important interschool matches with Wellington, Rugby, Marlborough, Clifton or Oundle. Smaller schools were contemptuously treated to the second XV and players like me who could rough it. But I had been caught visiting my parents in Kashmir when the

A chap called Colson, glowing with health and determination.

9

war broke out in 1939 and hadn't been near a rugger ball for over a year.

"Never mind, you'll soon pick it up again. Are you fit?"

"Not very."

"Soon will be. I'll put you down."

"I haven't any gear." My last desperate ploy.

"Cotton's down the Turl. Fix you up in no time. Keep an eye on the notice board in the Chapel arch," and he was gone and I was down to play rugger. I later learnt the saying that in college rugby it's a brave man who goes near the ball, it's an idiot who picks it up. But nothing had prepared me, unpractised and unfit, for my initiation, a neat hand written note on O.U.R.F.C. paper inviting me to report to the Iffley Road ground for a Freshman's Trial.

Trial was a good word. I found myself on the appointed day shivering amongst an assortment of about forty ferocious looking young warriors eager to prove their credentials for inclusion in the University team. Sides were picked and positions allocated and, in next to no time, I was heaving and sweating under a pile of forwards or being confronted by bone shaking tackles and generally being as bruised and battered as can only happen in a scratch match among total strangers. Players were exchanged at regular intervals and sometimes switched to the other side to get some sort of even balance.

Since I seemed to spend most of my time beneath a pile of bodies I doubt if the selectors who were watching would have seen me too often but fortunately, after about half an hour, I emerged from the mud for long enough to be spotted and replaced. My brief moment of glory was over and I trudged back to college, bloodied but unbowed, to wallow in a boiling bath. I was surprised to read later in the Oxford Magazine that the Freshman's Trial "had shown there was considerable and unexpected new talent available." And indeed I suppose it was so because, in a subsequent full trial match, two of my fellow freshmen, Somner and E.M. Lock, were called into service. Colson's influence was clear because in addition to the two newcomers there were five other Trinity men on show including another Old Cheltonian, Clive Wilkinson together with Messrs

Convocation House where we were matriculated.

The view from my room of old Durham College, the oldest part of the College.

My room, were the three sets of double windows directly above the door into the College Hall, which has the founders bust over it.

The freshman's photograph Michaelmas 1940.
Back Row: Lugg, Van Zwanenberg, Temple-Carrington, Bond, Darlington, Reinhold, Dawson, Aiers, Spinney
Centre Row: Mathew, Wade, Magee, Harper-Nelson, Margesson, E.M. Lock, Marsh, Eyre, Bolton, Oliphant, Curtis
Front Row: Smith, Shoeten-Sack, Staveley, Somner, Williams, Mollison, Dixon, M.E. Lock, Carton-Kelly, Drury
Absent: Sotheron-Estcourt, St. John, Engelbach, Parker, Stephens, Pilkington.

Parker, Kaye and Rampton. Another school contemporary of mine, Bill Bayliss of Wadham subsequently made the University team. For my part I turned out four or five more times for the college, enjoyed the Guiness shandy after the games but decided that my bleeding nose was better kept out of it in future. Besides other interests had come to occupy my time. The first of these was to become an official member of the University by being Matriculated. This involved dressing up in a dark suit -sub-fusc officially - with white shirt, winged collar, and white bow tie with mortar board and commoners short gown to be paraded by the Dean and shepherded across to the Sheldonian Theatre. From there we were ushered to the Bodleian Library to be presented to the Vice Chancellor holding court in Convocation House. Presumably because there were so many of us, we were matriculated in groups. We raised our caps, bowed politely, listened to the traditional Latin induction formula and trooped out. As we did so we were passed by a platoon of Royal Corps of Signals Officer Cadets crunching across the quad in battle-dress, boots and gaiters but wearing their black undergraduate gowns. Apparently a university course was part of their training to be officers.

There were twenty-nine of us from Trinity and, when one looks back at the list of names and schools, it is obvious why we were, on the whole, such a close knit little community because we all came from the same sort of predominantly middle-class backgrounds. These, of course, were the days when our fond parents had to foot the bills and the only financial assistance a student could get was by winning a scholarship. These were my fellow freshmen:- M.F. Dixon (Ampleforth), I.M. Mollison (Rugby), M.R. Williams (Oundle), J.E. Somner (Christ's Hospital), A.G. Eyre (King's School, Canterbury), C.D. Oliphant (Edinburgh Academy), M.S. Staveley (Stamford), D.L. Reinhold (Wellington), D.H. Marsh and S. Bolton (Harrow), L.D. Carton-Kelly (Downside), J.H. Darlington (Shrewsbury), E.L. Magee (Giggleswick), D.B. Dawson (Bradfield), R.A.B. Drury (Gresham's), P.S. Engelbach (Tonbridge), E.M. Lock (King's School, Canterbury), M.E. Lock (Shrewsbury), N.R.F. Mathew (Lancing), C.L. Pilkington (Eton), V. St John (Felsted), E.L.N.

Shoeten-Sack (King's College School), E.G.A. Sotheron-Estcourt (Harrow), A.G. Temple-Carrington (Radley), D. Van Zwannenberg (Shrewsbury), M.R. Curtis (Malvern), D.P. Aiers (Stationers Company School), and F. Margesson (Eton).

The next event to take place after Matriculation was to be appointed to a course of study. The Don in College responsible for this sort of guidance was known as one's moral tutor. In my case this was the kindly and revered person of Tommy Higham, who was held in high academic awe for his prowess as the University Orator which entailed officiating at all major University functions such as the conferring of honorary degrees on visiting dignitaries and extolling their virtues in elegant and elegaic Latin. I had expressed a wish to study English as I had youthful ambitions to be a writer, but this was regarded as rather frivolous and I was firmly entered upon the course known as PPE:- Politics, Philosophy and Economics. Politics seemed an interesting course of study especially as the lecturers included G.D.H. Cole whose writings were much admired at the time. As for Philosophy, I was prepared to argue over whether I knew or only believed that something existed and looked forward to the intellectual challenges with which I might be confronted. But Economics floored me and this was to be my main course of study in my first term. In spite of the encouragement of friends like Max Stamp I couldn't absorb the basic arguments, partly because it seemed to involve a mathematical talent which I never had. So my first term found me academically at sea. After about five weeks of stammering incomprehension, my tutor sent a note to the college suggesting that I take some other course of study. With some reluctance I was allowed to switch to the English school and was assigned to the tutelage of Nevill Coghill.

Your tutor was the centre of your academic life. If you were lucky you were assigned to someone kindly and compatible who would tolerate you and provide friendly guidance and instruction. Nevill Coghill was just such a person. He was large and soft spoken. His room in Exeter College was comfortable and invitingly untidy. Crossed oars on his wall advertised his youthful prowess and an old-fashioned trumpet-horned gramophone in the corner expressed his gentle conservatism. I am sure he thought me a poor student, which indeed I was, but we were, however, drawn together by a mutual and consuming interest in the theatre which would develope and grow with time. Through him I met Glynne Wickham with whom I came to establish a close and happy working relationship.

Margaret Rawlings, who knew and encouraged my love of the theatre, had launched her own career from the University Dramatic Society - the OUDS - and had told me that I must join. She was a friend of my sister's and, from the time I first met her when she was starring in "The Flashing Stream" in London, I thought that she was the most sensuously glamourous creature I had ever met. Not only that but she was wicked! Her friend Monica Stirling knew her well and regaled us with tales of Margaret's terrible deeds. She had been an "enfant terrible" at Oxford. When she married Gabriel Toyne she wore a scarlet wedding dress. She was having an affair with the author Charles Morgan. She had a white bear-skin rug in front of her fireplace and there were tales of erotic beatings with lilac branches. Never can a woman have been so demonised by her dearest friend and thus so glamourised in the eyes of this young worshipping acolyte. She was also highly intelligent and extremely kind and generous. In the Summer of 1940 she helped me swot for my forthcoming college entrance exam, coaching me in Shakespeare, reading the sonnets in that wonderful sonorous voice with its quirky intonation, and acting her famous role of Charmian for an enthralled audience of one. She also did Cleopatra's death scene, Lady MacBeth, Rosalind, Cordelia, Titania, and the Seven Ages of Man. I'm sure that if I could have taken her with me I could have passed the exam. But then, by God, I'd have ended up in Balliol! But, of course, I had to join the OUDS.

The OUDS came to me with another knock on the door and the entry of a slim ginger haired young man named Reginald Barr. He explained to me that he was the President of the College Dramatic Society and was planning to do a combined production with the Christ Church Dramatic Society at the end of this term or early in the next. When I asked about the OUDS,

Nevill Coghill

Trinity College Chapel
The rooms shared by Reggie Barr & A.G. Macpherson are directly above the doors.

he explained that the society had gone broke and no longer existed as such. However Nevill Coghill, as the senior member, had devised an organisation called the Friends of the OUDS with the avowed intention of paying off the OUDS debt by putting on a series of productions. It seemed a fairly blatant method of dodging the creditors but meant that university productions would go ahead but in a much more modest fashion. The trouble had been that the pre-war OUDS had become something of a casting agency for the West End. Ambitious would-be actors had engineered the Society into employing professional actors in leading roles and leading directors to put the shows together. As a result they had grossly overspent their budgets. In addition there had been a large social membership which, it seemed, had been a drain rather than a help to the organisation.

A further surprise was that Oxford had neither a Chair of Drama nor a theatre. In peacetime the principal annual productions had traditionally taken place in the garden of one of the colleges. Magdalen College garden was still said to be recovering from the Reinhardt production of a "A Midsummer Night's Dream" in which the cast had included real deer and rabbits. The alternative setting was the expensive option of hiring the huge New Theatre. Now the blackout had put paid to the open air performances at night and finance had closed down the other.

Having registered my enthusiastic interest in university theatre, I was invited to come to Reggie's room to read for a part in "Othello". Reggie shared his sitting room with A.G. MacPherson, which, beside being remarkably spacious, had the added attraction of a chimney piece carved by Grinling Gibbons. With a pair of windows looking out over the front quad and another onto the Chapel quad it seemed the most desirable residence in the college. It was generally assumed that Reggie had been allotted these quarters because he was the organ scholar and therefore required accomodation close to the chapel. He had catholic tastes in music and, after being persuaded that there was a genuine fugue in the Benny Goodman version of "Sing, Sing, Sing", he became quite a knowledgable student of

Stanley Parker's cover for The Cherwell

Michael Meyer (front row, centre) in 1940. Editor of The Cherwell and "something of a collector's piece".

jazz. Some time later he took to introducing some of the less strident pieces by Duke Ellington such as "Solitude" and "Mood Indigo" into his recessional voluntaries after the chapel service which drew some quizzical looks from the Chaplain, Austin Farrer, but no complaints. In later months, jazz was to play a considerable part in our social calendar. In the meantime I had been duly enrolled in the Friends of the OUDS.

I still wanted to write and the opportunity came when the undergraduate magazine "The Cherwell" resumed publication on October 19th under the editorship of Michael Meyer. The Oxford Magazine welcomed its return with its attractive cover designed by Stanley Parker and called it "much improved except for the proof reading". Of most interest to me was its announcement of a short story competition. A couple of years earlier I had surprised everyone by winning the school poetry prize with a sonnet called "Christmas á la Mode" about Jews and Arabs shooting each other in the Holy Land. Cecil Day-Lewis had been the judge and it was duly published in the school magazine. For the Cherwell competition I wrote a topical piece about a London spiv smuggling a stolen jewel to America under the guise of a child refugee. It was written in the style of Damon Runyon who, with the American writers James Thurber, H. Allen Smith and S.J. Perelman, was enjoying almost cult status among us.

On 14th November I happily read, "there were over 20 entries for the Short Story competition. Most of the entries were of the boy meets girl variety, though there was a surprising number of crime stories. J. Harper-Nelson's Bunyanian (sic!) effort "The Child Lover" seemed slightly ahead of all the others and we have awarded it the first prize of a book to the value of 7/6". So, for the first time, I had achieved publication in more or less open competition. Anyway it was a step up from the school magazine. My instant admiration for Michael Meyer's excellent judgement was enhanced by the fact that he is the only person I ever met who had a full blue for real tennis which elevated him, in my view, to something of a collector's piece.

October was a busy month. Apart from all the business of settling into college there were numerous distractions. The local theatre consisted of the Playhouse which was running weekly repertory under the direction of Julian d'Albie, and the New Theatre in George street which hosted a succession of Number One tours. The London blitz had certainly benefitted the provinces in this respect. For example, by the end of the month we had seen variety with Oliver Wakefield and Hutch, Lupino Lane in "Me and My Girl", and Emlyn Williams, Angela Baddeley and Anthony Ireland in "The Light of Heart". At the Playhouse they had done very good versions of a fairly safe repertoire, "Berkeley Square", "Goodness How Sad", "Yes and No", and "Gaslight". Here too the closing of the West End theatres enabled the company to include John Byron, Rosemary Scott, Winifred Evans, Pamela Brown, Angela Wyndham-Lewis, Peter Ashmore, Peter Copley, Nora Nicholson, Sigrid Landstad, and Anthony Woodruff. Later they would be joined by John Moffat and Rosalie Crutchley. So, in spite of the University turning a blind eye, there was considerable theatrical activity. Perhaps it was because of this that the Oxford Union decided to debate the establishment of a Chair of Drama. The distinguished actor Leslie Banks, who I had seen creating the title role in "Goodbye Mr Chips" at the lovely old Shaftesbury Theatre before it was destroyed in the bombing, came to propose the motion. In the afternoon, before the debate, he was the guest of a Friends of the OUDS reception hosted by Nevill Coghill.

The motion was "That this House would welcome an extension of the scheme of National Theatres and the establishment of a Chair of Drama in Oxford." We all crowded into the Union debating chamber to hear Leslie Banks' impressive speech followed by an extremely witty contribution by A.G. MacDonnell leading the opposition. The drama critic James Agate opposed the motion with a rambling speech that seemed to be more about the establishment of a National Theatre than the Chair of Drama. He summarised his own contribution in his diary entry the next day, October 25th.

"Spoke at the Union. The motion was the establishment of a chair of drama at Oxford, proposed by Leslie Banks and opposed by A.G. MacDonnell. One of the undergraduates made the excellent point that you can't mix dead languages and living drama, and that if Oxford dons were allowed to contact the living drama they would kill it. I summed up the debate with a distinct bias against the whole business of National Theatres. Talking about idealists and the harm they do, I suggested that the proper way to deal with the C.P. Scotts is to behead them in the morning, give them an Abbey funeral in the afternoon, and canonise them in the evening. So with the proposed Chair of Drama. Establish it in the morning, chop it up for firewood in the afternoon, and in the evening make a bonfire of it on the steps of the Martyr's Memorial. `What about the blackout?' piped some vulgar little boy. The motion was carried handsomely, 231 votes to 89."

Agate ended his speech with a flourish of a walking stick which he claimed had belonged to Hogarth but, as the Cherwell report said,"whether it was intended to drive us into the Ayes lobby or the Noes we were not quite clear." Which goes to show that, even with the remoteness of years, my impression that Mr Agate had missed the point was probably right. However the Chair of Drama was never established. The following term The Cherwell published my article titled "Let Us Revive Our Theatre" arising from this debate but Glynne Wickham had to wait many years and go to Bristol to realise what had been a mutual dream back in 1940.

CHAPTER TWO

Having a room over the college hall had its advantages. First it was conveniently close when a last minute dash had to be made to be in time for breakfast. Secondly, when I eventually assembled my drum kit for some practice, I had no-one above or below me to annoy and only David Marsh and Paddy Engelbach along the corridor. From my windows I looked onto the Chapel quad with the back of the Garden quad buildings on my left, the Chapel on my right and, across the quad in front of me the oldest part of the college which housed the Bursar's office and the old library. This was the original Durham College, founded in the 13th century by the Bishop of Durham who is reputed to have initiated the feud with the college next door by throwing stones at John de Balliol's window. The college became dedicated to the Holy and Undivided Trinity in 1560 under the auspices of Sir Thomas Pope whose portrait hung in the place of honour in the Hall above the High Table. Below it hung a portrait of his wife, the Lady Elizabeth, whose name was traditionally perpetuated on the bows of the college first VIII racing shell.

For seven hundred years this place had been inhabited by monks and scholars and common students, most of whom had gone their various ways in unremarkable and unrecorded fashion, except in some college archive or if someone remembered to name them in a book. Now I was a part of this strange structure, enclosed within it's ancient walls, inheriting it's traditions, until I too passed on to make whatever mark I might on the world outside. And I knew, as I looked across at that old grey building, that what I did here and who I met would mark me for life and no matter where I went in the world I would be drawn back in mind if not in body. From the beginning I was conscious of this magnetism. It was something I had only previously felt in the old Abbey church in Iona near my family home in the Isle of Mull. If it is true that my maternal grandmother was sired by Sir Colin Campbell, fresh from his triumphs at Balaklava and Lucknow and glad to accept the favours of the ladies of the lands through which he passed, then I too have Campbell blood and that strain of second sight that instinctively absorbs one into the community of spirits past.

However it was the community of spirits present that had to occupy my mind as a freshman and a very conformist community it was too. The communal centre of undergraduate life was the JCR -the Junior Common Room. Situated on the first floor of staircase 7 in the New buildings facing the front quadrangle, it provided a haven for those who got there early enough to loll in front of the large coke brazier in the fireplace and read the papers. When fuel was short and the weather cold it was a much sought after refuge.

The interests of the undergraduates were supposed to be represented by the JCR committee which was elected each term by those who could be bothered or remembered to attend the meeting. Apart from a President, Secretary and Treasurer, the most important members were the Food committee who bore the brunt of any complaints and were expected to convey them to the Domestic Bursar. It required exceptionally public-spirited young men to fill these positions but for those of us lower down on the scale of responsibility there were such delightful appointments to be filled such as Master of the Rolls, whose duty was to ensure an adequate supply of lavatory paper, Rear Admiral whose duties involved the cleanliness and hygiene of the lavatories in question, and the Garden Boy whose duties were defined as "to determine the sex of the college tortoise and find a suitable mate." I think I filled all of these various posts at some time or another although I never managed to find the college tortoise and have never been entirely convinced that there was one.

As freshmen we dutifully attended the inaugural AGM of

The JCR in 1958. Except for the electric fire and the "Daily Herald" it hadn't changed much since 1940.

the Michaelmas Term and duly elected Jack Rampton as President, Straghan Secretary, Colson and Rampton Captain and Secretary of Rugger, Partridge and Evans Hockey, Straghan Soccer, Rampton Squash, Reinhold Athletics, Taylor Garden Boy, Wilkinson Rear Admiral, Du Santoy, Marten, Murray and Davenport Food Committee and the post of Master of the Rolls appears to have been left vacant. With the exception of Reinhold, these were mostly second and third year men and we were greatly impressed with their apparent poise and sophistication. Paddy Engelbach wondered if he was ever going to make the grade.

"When I was in the bath house last night, the chap in the next door bathroom was whistling Mozart," he said.

I managed to reassure him by telling him that it was pretty erudite of him to have known it was Mozart. We were sitting in Paddy's room, David Marsh, Vernon St John and I, discussing the happenings of the day before grabbing our gowns and clattering down stairs to pass under the eagle eye of Cadman on our way into hall for dinner. We had already learnt that Cadman, as Head Scout, was the judge and arbiter of correct dress for meals and had no compunction about refusing admission to anyone he thought was improperly dressed, especially in the evening when gowns had to be worn.

We had been detailed off into squads for ARP duties but were still a bit vague about what we had to do. In spite of the general belief that Oxford had been declared an Open City, which meant it was basically undefended and a centre for hospitals and non-combatant activities, we still had some air raid precautions to observe. The air raid shelters designated for the college were the cellars beneath the buttery and kitchen but, with an air of pragmatic nonchalance, it was decreed that undergraduates should use the basement of the New Bodleian as access to the college cellars "was not convenient". We strongly suspected that this was to preserve the college wine stocks which Philip Landon, the Bursar, would undoubtedly have regarded as more valuable than an undergraduate.

We were divided into three divisions. The First Division covered the front quad and its surrounding buildings, the Third

Cadman, posed appropriately outside the President's lodging.

Division the Garden quad and we of the Second Division were responsible for the protection of the Chapel, Chapel quad, Staircase 10, the Tower, kitchens, bathrooms and lavatories. To do this we were assigned into four squads. Squad A consisted of Curtis, Dawson, Davies, Moss, Partridge, Marsh, Barr and Magee and were to operate the hoses. Squad B, armed with stirrup pumps were Evans, E.M. Lock, St John, Straghan, Drury, Engelbach and myself. Squad C with ladders were Staveley, Shoeten-Sack, Kaye, MacPherson, Bolton, Van Zwannenberg, and M.E. Lock, while D Squad of Rice-Oxley, Carton-Kelly, Wilkinson, Bond, Parker, R.G. Smith, Gurney, Campbell-Colquhoun, Wade and Stephens were armed with shovels. Each division was divided into sections consisting of one or two men from each squad so that, in theory, there would be hose-men, stirrup pump men, chaps with ladders and chaps with shovels to dig us out if all else failed. Those of us detailed for duty had to be in college from 6 p.m. onwards and, if there was an air raid alert, to remain up and fully dressed until the All Clear. On the alert, two members of the section were to go up onto the top of the chapel tower to be relieved every hour if possible. It was this last command that was to be the cause, if not the excuse, for some acts that incurred official disapproval and wrath.

To get to the top of the chapel tower it was necessary to go through the room which contained the machinery that operated the clock and, more importantly, the clock's bell. The temptation to make the clock strike thirteen at midnight proved too much for some, but the most confusion could be caused in the early morning when a long night's watch could be enlivened by adding a couple of chimes to four or five o'clock and watching the panicked rush for baths and breakfast. Then there were the inveterate Balliol baiters who took a supply of refreshment in bottles to help to pass the time and threw the empties with a satisfactory crash onto the Balliol green-house below.

There were also problems caused by the fact that members of other colleges resided in Trinity because their own college accomodation had been requisitioned for some wartime activity. Some guests from Keble College got into trouble in March 1941. R.G. Storey was cautioned for being absent from ARP duty and

Trinity's static water tank outside the library was made into an attractive rose garden by President Weaver

J.G. Thomas "while on fire-watching duty, poured water down chimney causing extensive damage in the Tower room." Reggie Barr and MacPherson had their fire burning when the deluge descended filling their room with a mixture of hot soot, steam and ash. Unfortunately the punishment for this misdemeanour is not recorded but probably included paying for the damage since, on the occasion when the Dean of Balliol inadvertently left his lights on without blacking out his windows, and was subjected to a barrage of coal and bottles thrown from the back of Staircase 11, the attacker was "cautioned and made responsible for damages (with such assistance as he could get from unidentified accomplices)". The college agreed to pay four pounds four shillings and five pence. The principal assailant had been Simon Partridge who had been caught in the act by the Dean of Balliol himself who had seen the assault on his window and had walked through the door between the colleges to remonstrate with the attackers. His accomplice, whose name was supplied to the Dean, was C.G. Byrde, which cost him the damages but no doubt Simon paid his share.

The Dean's easy access to Trinity came about because all the gates and doors between the colleges were left unlocked in case of fire. The Auxiliary Fire Service Unit for the Trinity, Balliol, St John's complex was based in Trinity under the command of one Hodgens of Balliol. They held regular drills in the front quad displaying skills with their high-powered hoses that would have given them a distinct advantage should hostilities with Trinity have broken out. It might even be claimed that Balliol invented the idea of the water cannon. To make sure that the water didn't run out if the mains supply should be cut, each College was supplied with a large static water tank containing several thousand gallons of reserve water. In Trinity this was situated outside the College library and, in due course, was made the centre of an attractive rose garden by President Weaver.

It may seem strange that so much fire-watching was necessary. The reason was simply that Oxford, being close to the middle of southern England, was inevitably affected by the formations of bombers that were continually heading for Birmingham and the industrial heartlands, quite apart from the chance that the Morris Motor works at Cowley might be raided one night and the University collect some of the strays. So we spent quite a few hours gazing over the moonlit roof tops. On a pleasant night it was a beautiful sight but tempered with the knowledge that the wavering glow that lit the horizon over London to the East or Birmingham to the West meant that possibly relatives and friends were going through yet another night of fear and discomfort.

The college authorities, presumably in an effort to retain as much normality as possible, were not unduly sympathetic to the inconveniences of the war. In September, E.de V. Bolton and C.V.I. Snell were recorded as having been fined one pound each for "incompetence and trouble to staff" because they had arrived back from Guildford at one-thirty-five a.m. "having been held up a good deal by air raids". The unfortunate Hodgens of Balliol, who was to organise our auxiliary fire fighters, was noted as having "arrived in college for the first time at 1-40 a.m. with overcoat over AFS uniform. Said he had caught train at 7-40 from London, his departure being delayed by tidying up duties as Auxiliary Fireman. Train held up the whole way. Severely cautioned and warned to catch earlier trains in future." There appears to have been little recognition that, at this time in our history, Great Britain was standing alone against Germany. The Americans had not yet been forced in by the Japanese and Russia was still on the side of the Germans, not having been attacked. The idea that an Auxiliary Fireman, operationally involved in the London blitz, might want to clean up before handing over his duties and reporting to the college seems not to have entered anyone's head.

So domestically we were more or less safe in our beds if not necessarily fire-proof. On staircase 11 we had an advantage in our proximity to the kitchen. North was able to collect a sufficient supply of boiling water for all of his "gentlemen's" shaving requirements. He also managed to acquire a large pot of tea, enough for all those who needed a cup to waken them. If you were quick there was just time to rush to the bath-house before dressing, otherwise it was a case of pulling on one's clothes as quickly as possible and dashing down to the Hall for breakfast.

Undergraduate clothes were almost a uniform; grey flannel trousers, shirt and tie, pullover, tweed sports jacket, brown or black lace-up shoes. Shirts with collars attached were worn only for sports such as cricket so that studs had to be fiddled with, front and back. Van Heusen shirts were popular because they boasted a semi-stiff collar which kept its shape longer and you got two with each shirt. Underwear consisted of woollen vests with short sleeves and three buttons at the neck although those of us who had been overseas used sleeveless singlets by Aertex. Underpants looked like shorts with fly-button fronts and tape loops through which the Y-shaped part of the braces were threaded before being buttoned to the trousers back and front. The braces were usually striped elastic and, in many ways, gave more comfort at the waist than the later craze for belts. Those who had trousers with loops through which a belt could be worn tended to choose to wear an old neck tie, usually in school or club colours. Socks were held up by suspenders which hung down from garters worn below the knee. Tricks learnt at school meant that trousers and underpants or shirts and vests could be pulled on quickly as single units. The only area of non-conformity in dress came with the accessories. A six foot long woollen scarf in college colours was almost invariably wound round the neck with the ends dangling down to the knees but I embellished this with a pair of leopard skin gauntlets that I had brought from Kashmir and, in colder weather, I affected a camel hair overcoat worn with theatrical nonchalance over the shoulders like a cape. Most of us had some kind of trench coat for the rain but I don't remember any of us wearing hats. The necessity to wear gowns for tutorials, lectures and to enter libraries meant that these were carried over the arm although some wore them habitually as part of their daily dress. The rule that gowns had to be worn out of college in the evening was almost totally ignored.

Officially I believe that there was a college roll call at eight every morning which I don't remember ever having attended but I gathered that this was when the scouts from each staircase reported whether indeed their charges had spent the night in their rooms. Failure to do so without permission meant a visit to the Dean. Indeed it was his scout, Gynes, who reported Derek Morphett for having a guest sleeping on his sofa. He was an airman on 36 hours leave and it was a Saturday night. Derek told the Dean that he had been trying to get a room for his friend. However he had come in with his guest at 1-40 a.m.and had apparently been offered one of several rooms that had been made ready for a conference. He was fined ten shillings. Later in the term, A.R. Taylor had his cousin, also an airman on short leave, sleeping on a sofa in his room but was only cautioned and "adjured to obtain leave of the Dean in course of such proceedings."

The monastic origins of the foundation were clearly continued in the rules concerning women who could only be entertained in college during day time and had to be out of the gates by 7 p.m. Strangely women did not feature largely in our lives except as casual acquaintances. The University girls kept to themselves and most of those we knew were the day girls known as Home Students (later to become St Hugh's). There were also the girls of Westfield College, London, who had been evacuated to Oxford for the duration and seemed to be more forthcoming.

Sex within the college rarely raised its ugly head, not least because without sporting one's oak, there was always the danger of an enthusiastic neighbour bursting in ostensibly to borrow a book but more probably out of jealousy or curiosity. Our doors were never locked and the rules of decorum, which still prevailed, made sporting one's oak a strictly academic activity. It was generally accepted that a man who sported his oak with a woman in his room was a cad, but one who did so with another man in his room was a bounder. For those whose lust knew no bounds there was a very pretty seventeen-year-old who worked in Taphouse's music shop next to Elliston's. She also taught dancing and in a brief moment of ambition I signed on and clumped away in the rehearsal room above the shop. But none of us ever managed to go solo as it were. Corinne Hunt knew her worth and played for safety in numbers.

Thoughts of females were far from our minds as we ran down the stairs to grab breakfast at the last tick of the clock.

The tables in Hall were lined up in four rows stretching up to the High Table which ran across the far end on its low dais beneath the portrait of the founder. The tables on the left nearest to the door were generally reckoned to be for the freshers. The table furthest to the right near the huge stone fireplace was the senior table where the scholars sat and from which the senior scholar present had to recite the Latin Grace before dinner. The tables were long oak refectory style with wooden benches to match. Meals were served by the Scouts supervised by the imperious presence of Cadman, the head Scout.

Wartime meals were somewhat inhibited by rationing. Ration books had to be handed in to the Domestic Bursar at the beginning of term. Some items, such as fresh eggs had already become rareties but I was never conscious of feeling that the meals were inadequate or that I was suffering from insuperable pangs of hunger. Breakfasts were bolstered by liberal helpings of porridge and milk. Fried bread or piggy toast featured frequently and a form of scrambled egg made from egg powder. There always seemed to be plenty of bread or toast made from the greyish bread which had been proclaimed as the National Loaf. Ray Peters, a cherubic young man who sat at our table, claimed that the loaf had been invented by his father on the soundest of scientific principles and that it was healthier and more nutritious than the bleached white bread to which we had been accustomed. In view of the fetish for whole meal, stone ground, and coarse grained bread that has developed since, he was probably right.

College luncheons were not compulsory so that anyone having lunch had to sign on a slip of paper placed on each table. Lunch, as provided by the college consisted of "commons"- soup, bread and cheese. This could be augmented according to one's means by helpings of salad, cold meat, serves of mashed potato and so on. Tankards of beer could be ordered from the Buttery. These extras were charged to our battels at the end of term. Paddy Engelbach had seen a Three Stooges comedy in which the three had drawn names out of a big Western hat to decide which girl each of them would date. The first drew Annabel, the second Claribel and the third triumphantly proclaimed "Stetson!". Paddy enjoyed this so much that he signed Stetson on the luncheon slip every day and was delighted to see an envelope addressed to Mr Stetson thrust into the letter rack in the porter's lodge at the end of term. He wondered how long it would be before Mr Stetson would be written off as a bad debt.

The most pleasurable meal of the day was afternoon tea. This was served in our rooms and consisted of such seasonal delights as hot buttered toast with honey, thinly cut cucumber sandwiches, crumpets and rich fruit cake brought decorously by our scout.

This was not necessarily a daily routine and had to be paid for as an extra. I believe that those who simply wanted to refuel with a cup of tea and a slice of cake could get it in Hall. Nevertheless this was our principal method of entertaining any female we wished to impress and also, for the sheer joy of it, we contrived to have regular tea parties in each others rooms where the conversation could range far wider than the restrictions of Hall where the mention of women or politics was forbidden on pain of being sconced.

Sconcing was a penalty rarely imposed during my time except in the nature of a challenge. It consisted of having to consume about two and a half pints of beer from a silver cup in one draught without the lips leaving the cup. Failure meant having to pay for a round of ale for the whole table. At the risk of being thought a bad sport, it was often easier to pay for the round than try to swallow the sconce and most of us, when challenged, did so.

Dinner in Hall was usually taken with reasonable decorum. Before dinner we used to gather round the door of the buttery to drink beer and chatter before being ordered to take our places by the ever-present Cadman. We would then clatter noisily to our chosen tables, clutching our tankards, to wait standing until the procession of Dons had proceeded to the High Table. An indecipherable mumble, presumably in Latin, would emanate from the area of the fireplace after which the statutory three course meal would be served by the scouts. Three courses had been decreed by Parliament as the maximum that could be served and, outside the college, the maximum that could be charged for a meal was five shillings. Of course this was only for the meal and most restaurants managed to find a whole host of extras or service charges to boost the ultimate bill. Still, at 1940 prices, five shillings wasn't a bad amount when one considers that places like the Regent Palace Hotel in London or the Beresford in Glasgow only charged 10/6 for bed and breakfast.

Once or twice a term a burst of high spirits would result in a barrage of bread being exchanged between rival tables. This seemed to be tolerated as long as nothing was broken and nothing hit the High Table. It was strange, considering their importance in the continuing life of the college, how insubstantial the Dons appeared to be from the viewpoint of the junior members. Michael Maclagan was the Dean. He was a hawk-faced, raw-boned Scot who always seemed to be in a hurry to be somewhere else. Philip Landon, an eminent lawyer and reputed mysogonist, held court at the far side of the Garden Quad with the air and countenance of a mediaeval prelate. As College Bursar he was credited as being largely responsible for the excellence of college food even in wartime. Austin Farrer, the college Chaplain, pale and cassocked, had a distinctly Anglo-Catholic air. Thomas Higham, as my moral tutor, was the only Don with whom I had any close personal contact. The college President, J.R.H. Weaver, lived in the President's lodgings, presided at Dinner on occasions, and invited undergraduates in rotation to a pleasant and civilised dinner followed by his excellent lantern slides of classical architecture. But, unless one of the Dons was one's personal tutor, there seemed to be little contact. Since my tutor was in Exeter, the Dons seemed, for the most part, to be shadowy figures in gowns wafting to and from the High Table and occasionally being threatened by flying bread. Altogether it is probable that our domestic arrangements were little different from those of previous or successive years. It seems that, to the relief of its adherents and the exasperation or fury of its critics, life at Oxford flows, like the Isis, with inexorable tranquility in peace or war.

The war intruded with a letter from sister Margaret in London telling me that the Chevron Club which faced St George's Square in Pimlico close to Dolphin Square had been bombed. The club catered for non-commissioned officers who had often witnessed my parades with our two spaniels Romeo and Flush for their obligatory duties. The letter I wrote in return is typical of the sort of high facetiousness in which we used to indulge.

"Dear Margaret,
The sad fate of the Chevron Club is a tragedy that has moved me into several lines of doggerel. The number of embarassed minutes I have stood under the baleful glares of the outraged occupants while Romeo performs or Flush makes up his mind are uncountable. I shall indeed miss the Chevron when I return. Herewith, without MORE ADO I will quote.
("What ho, chums, I see the page is ended", chortled he, but the lower fourth knew they could rely on him for a new and daring idea. "At last, I have it," he cried, running to the book. The gang stood round aghast while he slowly turned the page. What was on the other side? For the rest of this thrilling serial, order your next week's copy of THE TOPPER now. 2d at your local booksellers.)

> Alas the Chevron Club is gone
> Its members shall no more look on
> The painful efforts, sure but slow,
> Of masters Flush and Romeo.
> No more shall they with baleful eye
> Gaze down from their high perch on my
> Embarrassed promenade and stance
> Evading every passer's glance.
> Oh Hitler, Goering, Ribbentrop,
> What made you on the Chevron drop
> Your bomb, and thus reduce to dust
> This noble club - a fate unjust?
> And you, O Chevron, in our thanks
> We will promote you from the ranks

No longer Chevrons you shall grace
We'll put a Crown up in their place.
Both King and commoner must share
The deathly peril of the air,
But when you rise, as rise you must,
From your brave ruins, noble dust,
When we rebuild our gallant town
Let's have not "Chevron" but the "Crown".
Thanking yew.

I've got to produce an essay on Value on Thursday so there's work to be done.
John Smedley and a friend have arrived home on three days leave so I am going out to Dinner tonight at Woodstock.
I must stop now as I am going on a library crawl with another bloke who goes to the same tutorials. Love to Pamela (Ooh La La!)
With much love —"

The "thanking yew" was a reference to Cyril Fletcher, a popular comedian whose act consisted of a series of topical Odd Odes whose style I had copied.

CHAPTER THREE

The arrival of John Smedley was a sharp reminder that we were indeed at war. He was dressed in Naval uniform and was on survivor's leave. John's father had been a friend of my parents in Lahore where he had been the Editor of the Civil and Military Gazette, the paper on which Rudyard Kipling started his career. John and I had been playmates in Lahore and had been sent to the same prep school although he was a year younger. His mother took rooms in Cheltenham while John was there and looked after me when my parents were in India. Sunday lunch during term time was almost invariably roast lamb followed by chocolate Swiss roll with cream. After lunch, John and I would play with our trains or Dinky toys or toy soldiers, punctuated by bleats from his mother of "Do be quiet, John, Mother's got such a headache". This may well have explained why John was an only child.

Smedley senior was a rotund, jolly extrovert who enjoyed amateur dramatics and a good party. As a child in Lahore, I remember him showing us a film he had made for the children's Christmas party of Father Christmas, played by himself, arriving at the bungalow in a tonga, coming into the house and entering the drawing room. He projected this on a big paper screen and, as Father Christmas walked towards us on the film, he burst through the screen shouting "Merry Christmas, children!". It was a wonderful idea and gave me a terrible fright.

At prep school, John had taken after his father, growing plump and cheerful and playing Sir Joseph Porter in "H.M.S. Pinafore" and the villain in "Emil and the Detectives." We had lost touch when I went on to the college and he had gone off to train for the Merchant Navy. Now here he was knocking at my door having tracked me down through Margaret, looking like a younger version of his father and asking me to come out to see his parents.

On retirement, his father had bought the Bear Hotel in Woodstock, a beautiful old coaching inn near Blenheim Palace where his mother was in charge of the house-keeping and complaining about the servants.

John had joined the Blue Funnel line and was serving on the "Patroclus", which had been turned into a merchant cruiser for convoy escort work. She had been torpedoed off the the north of Ireland and John had spent eleven hours in the water before being scooped up in the loading net of a passing destroyer like some enormous fish. The ship's doctor had prescribed a tumbler of neat whisky to cure the lack of circulation in his blackened limbs which knocked him out cold so that by the time he awoke his circulation had been restored and he was heading home. His only regret, apart from losing his ship, was seeing his piano accordion sinking beneath the waves and his wallet with a hundred pounds of newly drawn pay floating away out of his reach. It was a salutory reminder that while we were enjoying our sybaritic existence in the confines of Trinity, others were out there risking their lives on our behalf.

Off we went to the Bear Hotel to renew old acquaintance and to celebrate John's survival. We decided to experiment. Since my parents were teetotallers and my only experience with alcohol had been the occasional cider and the odd half pint of beer, we thought we had better find out what everything tasted like. We started at the left hand end of the shelf behind the bar as we faced it with just a wee nip, a thimble full really, of each drink. Whisky, Brandy, Gin, Rum, Cointreau, Creme de Menthe, Benedictine, Drambuie, Cherry Brandy and on and on. I believe I got back to Trinity by taxi. I know that I folded my clothes with meticulous neatness on my bedside chair and that I was then hideously sick into my chamber pot before collapsing flat on my back on my bed. Which is how North found me in the morning. I had never been drunk before. Now I had been messily drunk and I was suffering. North seemed undismayed.

"Had a heavy night I see, Sir", he said.

I think I apologised for making such a mess.

"Never mind, sir, we'll soon get it cleaned up. Just you go and have a bath and get some black coffee and you'll feel better."

He was completely businesslike and matter-of-fact so that I realised that I was obviously not the first of North's "Gentlemen" to have thrown up. In Hall, I sought out Reggie Barr who, being in his second year, probably knew the score.

"Ten bob is the usual," he said,"Just give him ten bob and thank him for his trouble". And that was it.

I remembered that I had arranged to meet John in Elliston's for coffee and was glad to find him suffering as well. We went back to the Bear to revive ourselves on Brandy and Ginger Ale. John's father took it all in his stride but I felt some sympathy for Mrs Smedley if having an awful headache was like I was feeling.

John's arrival had a further salutory effect because it made me look at Oxford. Until he turned up I had concentrated my existence largely within the college. Now I became host and guide because John had never had time to look round Oxford either. So I showed off my newly learnt knowledge of names and places; that Turl Street, Broad Street, Cornmarket Street, High Street and Saint Giles were colloquially the Turl, the Broad, the Cornmarket, the High and the Giler, while pubs like the Lamb and Flag or the Eagle and Child were the Flam and the Bird and Baby. So we wandered round the University and looked at the buildings and gardens, down to Christ Church (carefully called The House), across Tom Quad past the Cathedral to the Broad Walk beside the meadows. We walked along the banks of the Cherwell to Magdalen Bridge and along the back lanes by Merton and Oriel, back into the High, past St Mary's and Queens and All Souls and, because there was a war on, there were no tourists, the streets were quiet, traffic was light and we could hear the sound of walking feet and the swish of passing bicycles.

We reminisced about our Indian childhood. His parents had a big old fashioned, thick walled and deep verandahed bungalow near the Racecourse in Lahore. My father had just been appointed Principal of the King Edward Medical College and we were living in a suite of rooms in Nedou's Hotel while a house was being built for him. John and I used to play in the big Nedou's garden watched by gossiping ayahs. It was a world of little excitements and curiosities. The day the hawk had got entangled with the kite strings and fell struggling to the ground in a tangle of string and coloured paper; hearing the lions roar at feeding time in the Zoo; and the slow creaking progress of the blind-folded buffalo walking round and round by the deep well in the Lawrence Gardens as the chain of buckets came dripping up from the depths to be emptied into the wooded trough that carried the water into the network of irrigation channels; of picnics by the Ravi, the wide river, among the cluster of palms reputedly grown from the excreta of Alexander's conquering army; of making sand castles in the dry sandy bed of the canal; "Come along, John, Mother's got such a headache." There was a photograph somewhere of the two of us, four and five year olds, in our solar topees looking like a pair of mushrooms. We remembered that, when they had finally left India, they had come to stay with us in the house my father had rented in Cheltenham and John had spoken with a strong chee-chee accent -Oh My!- and his excitement at seeing snow falling for the first time.

Reminiscences too of prep school, Cheltenham College Junior, with our rough grey shorts that gave us chaps in the winter and the masters we had liked or been afraid of - Slingsby, Tapsfield, Parker, Osborne, Hedges, Ross and Day-Lewis. Rusty Ross with his cigar shaped silver Riley sports car; Lionel Hedges driving round and round the school yard in an open Austin seven wearing a top hat playing Aunt Sally while we threw conkers at him; Day-Lewis frightening the life out of us in the junior dormitory telling us ghost stories with his face lighted with a green torch; Duggie Parker, slightly squiffed at prep, boasting of his wartime exploits in the navy, "When we were off the Dogger Bank —;" and the Headmaster's wife making sure that we knew that she was a Hugenot and encouraging us to act. Spud Landauer and I had worked the two Pathescope projectors to show silent movies in the library every Saturday night and John had worked the wind-up gramophone to provide the music. The choice was limited, the Chu Chin Chow Overture for the sinister bits, we showed "Metropolis" and "The White Hell of Pitz Palu", or the Washington Post for Snub Pollard, Charlie Chase and Chaplin. We didn't realise for ages what an amazing education in film we had given ourselves.

Then it was time for John to go back to sea, this time, he hoped, in a proper warship not a soft skinned merchantman. Good luck, keep dry and I never saw him again. Good-bye childhood.

Nevil's rooms "mercifully placed", now tucked behind the bushes below the big window.

St. John's College
Nevil Macready's rooms opened off the corner of the Quad. Philip Larkin was next to the right. All of this is now the College Library.

CHAPTER FOUR

> "There was a young fellow called Andrew Clair
> And he was the hell of a conjurair
> 'Cos he could throw his prick in the air
> While twisting and turning his balls.
> For they were large balls, LARGE BALLS,
> Balls as heavy as lead,
> And with a singular twist of his muscular wrist
> He could fling 'em right over his head."

I could hear the voices as I stepped through the wicket gate into the dim blue light of the St John's entrance. Across the quad, heading to the right, through another archway to a second quad and then head for the far right hand corner. Nevil Macready's instructions were clear and easy to follow. So too was the noise that emanated from his rooms, mercifully placed looking out onto the college garden. Mercifully, because the noise of undergraduate voices yelling what are euphemistically known as "rugby songs" was calculated to disturb the academic peace even in wartime.

> For he could bounce it on the ground
> And up in the air with a hell of a bound
> And onto the nose of his faithful hound
> While twisting and turning his balls...

The refrain was even noisier now, rending the darkness of the Oxford black-out. I shone my torch to find the door, pointing it upwards to check the number. I still felt guilty as I did so. Life in the London blitz had conditioned me to expect a plaintive cry of "Put that bloody light out." In the third week of term I still hadn't entirely come to terms with the peace of Oxford.

> Now he was walking down the street
> When little Miss Brown he chanced to meet
> While he was performing a hell of a feat
> Of twisting and turning his balls —

Nevil Macready had been at school with me and was a freshman at St John's but had clearly moved faster than I in establishing a circle of friends. This was partly because his room was a preferred location for the rowdier parties as it was just about as far away as possible from any of the college authorities.

> Little Miss Brown was quite distraught
> She swore she'd take the matter to court
> She didn't think a gentleman ought
> To go twisting and turning his balls...

I opened the door, blinking in the sudden light. The fate of Andrew Clair remained unproclaimed as a bellow from Nevil silenced the singers. "John, my dear chap, come in." He introduced me to a roomful of young men in various stages of early inebriation whose names I would instantly forget until I knew them better. Geoff, Esmund, Philip, Eddy, John, hands shaken and a pewter tankard of warm flat beer thrust into my hand. Nevil's sitting room was larger than mine in Trinity. A dining room sized table filled the middle of the room on which there was an assortment of beer in bottles and jugs and an HMV wind-up portable gramophone on the corner. My arrival had interrupted the singing so some-one put on a record. Ten inch 78s were scattered round in their paper covers proclaiming them to be HMV, Columbia or Parlophone. Some of them had the name of the shop from which they had been bought stamped on them, Acott's or Taphouses if they had been bought in Oxford. The music was the standard swing of the period, Benny Goodman, Artie Shaw, Bob Crosby, or Nevil's favourite Jimmy Lunceford playing "My Heart belongs to Daddy" sung by the sexy voice of Bea Wain.

So the beer would flow and the records spin until somebody decided it was time for another song.

Getting drunk at Oxford parties was rather like a tribal ritual or initiation. It was expected of you. There were those who pretended to be drunk earlier than they were in order to make an honourable escape. There were others who could nose out a party for exactly the opposite reason. One evening the door of Nevil's room burst open to reveal a slightly dishevelled but indubitably drunk young man.

"Cornwell of Jesus!" he shouted.

"Throw him out!", someone cried.

"Have his trousers," called another.

"Have them you may," replied Cornwell with drunken dignity,"but it will cost you a beer."

There was a brief struggle as his trousers were removed.

"I think he's a stout fellow," Nevil proclaimed, "Give the man a beer".

The interloper turned out to be one Roger Cornwell of Jesus College who later swore that he had crawled back to his college that night on all fours and therefore, considering himself to constitute vehicular traffic, had stopped at the traffic lights at the corner of the Cornmarket and the Broad until they went to green. As you may surmise, he was reading Law and became one of our regular gathering. He has fixed himself in my memory by announcing that his family crest was "a sloth dormant on a field of love lies bleeding with the motto Do Nothing Till You Hear From Me". I thought it was a pretty idea. Years later I met his brother Brian in Aden and Nairobi where he called me in urgently off an army exercise in which I was engaged to meet Sandy Wilson, an old friend of Oxford days whose successful musical "The Boy Friend" had been expanded from one of the sketches he had written for our revue "Oxford Circus".

After that first party I stumbled out into the sudden dark, groped my way round two quads, walked very straight past the porter's lodge, out through the wicket gate, turn left, head for the corner by Balliol. A small cluster of figures was facing the Martyr's Memorial. They were peeing. In a couple of terms one of them would boast that he had peed on every prominent building in Oxford including the Proctor's bicycle outside the Clarendon building. The rituals of the Oxford black-out.

In fact drinking within college was the official policy. All pubs and bars were out of bounds to undergraduates which did not decrease their popularity but merely added the zest of danger to their use. For the socially superior or ambitious, the Randolph Hotel at the corner of Beaumont Street and the Giler, or the Mitre at the junction of the Turl and the High were the places to be seen. The Gloucester Arms at the back of the Playhouse Theatre was the favoured resort of the repertory actors. Among our favourites were the tiny Turf off Queen's Lane on the way down to New College, which boasted the fastest shove-halfpenny board in England; the Flam - the Lamb and Flag - next to St John's and the Bird and Baby (the Eagle and Child) across the road. Then there was the Welsh Pony down beside the buses on the edge of Gloucester Green. For some unknown reason this closed an hour later than the other pubs and therefore became the final port of call for the roisterers. It also served fish and chips. It was here that Geoff Liebens proclaimed "the piece of cod that passeth all understanding" and bravely called the assembled boozers to order while he performed the ceremonial dropping of a chip. He had a bet that it could be heard landing.

The person responsible for policing this policy of prohibition was the University Proctor supported by a roster of Pro-Proctors and a small squad of enforcers called Bulldogs or Bullers.

Winding its nightly way through the list of pubs went the duty Pro-Proctor with his pair of attendant Bullers. He wore academic dress, sub-fusc, gown and cap - the mediaeval mortar board. The Bullers, who were recruited from the ranks of the staffs of the colleges, wore blue suits and bowler hats. This little entourage trailed round invoking the time-honoured ritual. The suspected undergraduate in the pub was approached, the cap politely raised, "Are you a member of this University, Sir?" Failure to admit it would be taken as a titular resignation and result in being instantly sent down.

"Your name and college please." A lie would incur greater wrath and retribution.

The Eagle and Child (1994) and the "Tiny Turf" have not changed greatly since 1940.

The Tiny Turf Tavern, what you see is almost all there is - no escape in 1941 - no shove ha'penny in 1994.

"May I suggest that you return to your college forthwith and confine your future drinking to that establishment."

Exit the blushing or sullen miscreant.

Most of the Pro-Proctors entered into the spirit of the thing by sticking to a regular circuit so that it was possible, with little inconvenience, to follow their progress and patronise a favourite watering hole after the procession had passed. However others regarded their role as that of true policemen and doubled back on their tracks to catch as many as possible. Various ingenious ruses were tried to avoid detection. Some carried cloth caps to attempt to resemble the locals. One man of resource is reputed to have vaulted the bar as the Proctor entered, stripped off his jacket and masqueraded as the barman. Sometimes sheer dogged patience could be applied to wait incommunicado until the Bullers gave up and moved on. Nevil spent nearly an hour in the lavatory of the Eagle and Child before being able to tip-toe away. Those who tried to run for it seldom succeeded. It was generally believed that the two Bullers consisted of one sprinter and one long distance runner. As college servants they probably enjoyed their moment of superiority and escape was difficult. However the Proctor's rule did not extend to college territory so that anyone who could reach college grounds was safe. St John's had an enclave in front of the gates and the steps into Queen's College were outside the gates in the High and therefore ranked as college territory and beyond the Proctor's grasp. Two fleeing undergraduates managed to make this sanctuary a short way ahead of the persuing Bullers. There they sat, watched by the waiting Bulldogs, until at one minute to midnight they rang the college bell, politely bade them Good-night and went in.

I was only progged once. The tiny Turf, apart from its shove-ha'penny board, is also reputed to be the smallest pub in England. It only had one door so there was no escape. Shove ha'penny rather than darts was our most popular pub game and it must have been a mixture of over-confidence or bravado that caused us to be so immersed in our game that the entry of the Pro-Proctor was almost unnoticed. It so happened that the Don on duty that night was my tutor Nevill Coghill. He had asked me for my name and college before recognising me, upon which he apologised profusely. I gathered that it was considered rather unsporting to prog your own students and the custom was to adopt an icy stare and totally ignore such a person while happily taking the names of the rest of the assembly. As Paddy Engelbach was fond of saying, the advantage of a Public School education is that it teaches one never to expect fair play, so such blatant favouritism was not considered out of place. The result was a visit to the Clarendon building in full academic rig to be fined three pounds for a first offence. Judging by the queue, the University coffers must have benefitted considerably from this particular regulation.

Midnight was the witching hour when all college gates were locked and late arrivals reported to the Dean which usually resulted in being inconveniently gated or confined to college for a number of days. So, after midnight, it was necessary to climb in. Access to Trinity was easiest from Parks Road by way of the St John's bicycle shed. Wartime fire precautions made life easy because the communicating doors between colleges were left open so that walls which once had to be climbed could now be walked through. Queen's College was reputed to be the most difficult to get in to and Magdalen the easiest because of the conveniently located spikes by a lamp post which were intended to keep climbers out but in fact helped them in. Passing policemen on the beat had been known to give a helping hand and those men who had digs down Walton Street near the back of Somerville were in constant demand to give the girls a leg up over the wall. It all added a spice of danger to our social life.

But social life was not confined to drunken parties in college or the bravado of pub crawling. For the majority of students social contacts were made in the coffee shops and small cafes that abounded. The dress circle bar of the Playhouse served coffee in the morning. Here you could find the stage struck hoping to make contact with real live professional actors. The actual real live professional actors, who came into the bar for their coffee break, were really only interested in trying to remember their lines and movements for the next play. In the days of weekly repertory there was a first night every Monday, a dress rehearsal every Sunday, and during the week, with matinees on Wednesday and Saturday, rehearsals for next week's play started at ten each morning. Anyone hoping to meet a real live actor under those conditions would probably find a distracted individual with a faraway look in his or her eye wondering how on earth they could be expected to remember fifty-two plays a year. Morning coffee could be had at the Randolph at a price. I think the only time I went there was when I was showing off to my sister and when Nevill Coghill once took me there for lunch. You couldn't say that the Randolph was a haunt of undergraduates. On the left hand side of the Cornmarket as you walked down from Magdalen Street was Fuller's Cafe, the home of Fuller's Walnut Cake. This was a coffee-flavoured sponge with cream filling and butter icing, decorated with walnuts and it melted in the mouth. No afternoon tea designed to impress a guest could be complete without one. For those who couldn't wait it could be eaten on the premises with a cup of freshly ground coffee which was still available despite wartime restrictions.

Not far away, down Saint Michael's Lane, almost opposite the Oxford Union, was the Beehive where you could get hot buttered toast dripping with honey and in the High there were various places tucked away down narrow passages such as the Town and Gown and The Noted, which were invariably overcrowded at night, but where it was usually possible to meet friends and squeeze in somehow. Further down the High towards Magdalen there was the Copper Kettle which dispensed decorous teas and coffees.

For those who were hungry it was possible to get a variety of things on toast at most of these but, unless you went into one of the hotels for a more formal meal, the favourite eating place at night was the Taj Mahal, upstairs in the Turl near the corner of Ship Street. Here you could get the most excellent curries, mild, hot, or chilli hot which brought you out in a sweat. By the middle of 1941 the rice had run out and boiled barley was substituted but this still remained the most popular restaurant for most of us. Because of the crowding one frequently had to queue until someone had finished and it was not uncommon to have to wait while the remains of the previous occupant's meal had been scraped off the table cloth with a spoon. But there is no doubt that the true social centre was Elliston's.

Elliston and Cavell was a department store which occupied almost the whole of the side of Magdalen Street from the corner with George Street to the Super Cinema. More or less encompassed by it was Taphouse's music shop where the lovely Corinne held court and where we spent many hours and far too much of our parent's money buying the latest swing records as soon as they were issued. On the first floor of Elliston's there was a cafe. Every store of the period had one, whether it was Cavendish House in Cheltenham or Peter Jones in London and they were all much the same. Rows of neat tables with fresh cloths on them, an EPNS sugar sifter and a four compartment cruet set stood on the middle of the table supporting a menu card and each table had four brown wooden upright chairs. As you entered Elliston's, the row of windows overlooking Magdalen Street and the Martyr's Memorial were on the right. The serving doors from which the neatly dressed and increasingly elderly waitresses emerged were on the left. Next to the mobile trolley which held the cups, saucers, and cutlery was a large Decca radiogram. This was loaded with an indeterminate set of 78s playing undistinguished and often indistinguishable tea-shop music. Every morning during term time from ten o'clock onwards, a straggle of scarf-trailing students would make its way up the stairs. Their intrusion into this oasis of middle-class calm for three periods of eight weeks each year must have been a tedious imposition for the regular clientele. Shock waves could be clearly seen when we infiltrated our own records into the pile on the auto-changer and turned the volume up so that the strains of Hearts and Flowers or the Strauss selection were suddenly shattered by Begin The Beguine or Blue Lou. It was usually possible to get two or three played before the management rushed in to restore sweetness and light music again.

At the far end of the room there was a larger round table with six or eight chairs which we used to try to commandeer. This was where you had to be if you wanted to know what was going on. It was where you went if you wanted to know where someone had got to. It was where the post mortems would take place on the previous night's activities, who did what with whom and where.

Here too we first mooted the idea of forming a University Rhythm Club, a euphemism for jazz to appease the sensitivities of the senior dons who would have to approve its registration. Here we plotted the lighting of Hamlet, floated the idea of forming a Theatre Guild, chose which films we were going to see and review, we hoped, for the Cherwell, and organised a variety of social and sometimes anti-social activities. It was a fluid assembly as people came and went to and from lectures and tutorials and ended with a general dispersal to libraries or college rooms to study for a few hours until the next get together.

Oxford life revolved to a great extent round the weekly tutorial at which an essay had to be read, based on the programme of books and research set by the tutor the previous week. The formula was the same. "Next week I'd like you to give your views on —, I suggest that you read —". A pile of books to be ploughed through and an immature opinion to be expressed. A thousand or so words to be read to a Don who had undoubtedly heard it all before. Nevill Coghill was always kind. "I'm interested in your opinion that Lycidas is simply doggerel, but do you not think —?"

Gently one would be steered into a tactful withdrawal, enabled to retire gracefully but never made to feel entirely inadequate.

The only centre, other than the pubs, where we occasionally used to meet was in the solid gentlemen's club comfort of the Oxford Union. This was more the happy hunting ground of the politically ambitious like Roy Jenkins who, although a Balliol man, was billeted in Trinity. Sometimes the debates were quite interesting, such as the one about the Chair of Drama, but none of us was politically inclined, except in a rather woolly haze of idealism engendered in us by the Spanish Civil War, Gollanz's Left Book Club and Hulton's crusading new magazine Picture Post.

The Oxford Union Society Debating Hall

The fact that the bar stayed open late on the Thursday debate nights was an added incentive but, when Derek Dowdall was forcibly ejected for offering Randolph Churchill a pint of beer and pouring it into his hat, it was purely a drunken rather than a political gesture.

University politics have always been suspect. The famous Union resolution not to fight for King and Country that so enraged people in the 1930s was typical of the rather empty grand standing that occasionally took place. The war put paid to all that anyway but there was still the seed of disruption. The University Labour Club had been hi-jacked by the left wing and allied itself with the Communists in opposing the war. The Soviet Union was allied with Germany at this time and the Communists were doing what they could to make sure that we lost. As a result the Government banned the publication of the Daily Worker newspaper which was the subject of some heated debate. We showed our anti-Communist sympathies by posting snowballs through the party's office door. The more orthodox left-of-centre organisation was the Democratic Socialist Club which played host to such luminaries as Clement Attlee, now no longer leader of His Majesty's Opposition but Deputy Prime Minister, Ellen Wilkinson, Professor Laski, Victor Gollanz and George Strauss. Apart from promising us a brave new world there was little any of them could say with the Germans still breathing heavily across the Channel.

We had in college a far more interesting contact with the Government in Frank Margesson whose father was Churchill's War Minister. Regrettably, far from being a source of exciting insights into Government policy or the conduct of the war, Frank's chief interest in his father's high office seemed to be in the discovery that His Majesty's Ministers did not have to obey the law so that, as a special treat, he was driven the wrong way round Trafalgar Square. Also there was the flamboyantly attractive red head Aileen Alexander who cut a swathe through a small platoon of eager suitors, whose father was also in Churchill's cabinet. But altogether there were too many other distractions.

The Ritz Cinema in George Street, the Super in Magdalen Street, the Electra in Queen's Street and the Scala, which screened foreign films, in Walton Street, lured us away from such serious matters as politics. And further out there was the Regal in Cowley and the New Cinema in Headington. Our standard of reviewing was one of academic superiority. "If you are fond of mules, you will like Twenty Mule Train," wrote Michael Meyer. "We have had films without women, films without men, and now we have a film without a plot'" I wrote of North-West Passage. Yet we weren't badly served as a random selection of films showing in one week in that Michaelmas term of 1940 shows. The Mortal Storm, French Without Tears, Blackmail, Rebecca, When The Daltons Rode and Strange Cargo. It was certainly possible to lead a very full social life and never go near a pub.

The Mortal Storm was one of a series of anti-Nazi films arising out of the war, presumably made to soften up American public opinion in the hope that the United States might take the plunge and actually get involved. A similar theme, the fervent Nazi who finds he has Jewish blood, was involved in "Heil Hitler", an American play which we were asked to help produce.

Edward Stirling had acquired the rights to it and needed a young cast to make it credible. Margaret had suggested that he contact me in Oxford.

How Margaret became involved in all this goes back to the Munich crisis of 1938. My two sisters, Margaret and Annabel, had just been installed in our new flat in the brand new Dolphin Square when they became involved with a circle of moderate left-wing intellectuals protesting against the Munich Agreement. They joined the crowd in Whitehall jeering and booing and chanting "Chamberpot Must Go". In the subsequent newsreel coverage, the sound of a cheering crowd recorded at a cup final in Wembley Stadium was used as Chamberlain waved his grubby piece of paper. It was an early lesson in media management. They used to meet in Martin Blake's bohemian flat off Buckingham Palace Road and brood about the League of Nations and the Spanish Civil War and Sanctions in a rather ineffective way while they fried sausages and drank cheap claret. There was Martin Blake, an idealistic school-master, Vandeleur Robinson who was private secretary to Philip Noel-Baker who was something or other in Parliament with the Labour Party and so had an aura of "inside information", and his wife, a very glamourous journalist called Clare Hollingworth. Clare achieved undying fame a year later by being on the spot when Hitler invaded Poland thus personally announcing the start of World War II. Then there was Leonard Whiteman, an assiduous theatre goer and man about town when he wasn't working in Lloyds Bank who had introduced two struggling young actresses he had somehow met at the Q Theatre, Pat Wood and Monica Stirling.

Monica, intense and highly intelligent, had been befriended by Margaret Rawlings to whom she subsequently introduced us. Her parents Edward Stirling and his wife, Hilda Vaughan, had lived for many years in Paris where they ran the English Theatre. By the outbreak of war, their other daughter Pamela was just beginning to make her mark in the French theatre and with small parts in films. She had achieved roles with the Comedie Francaise and with Louis Jouvet's company. The German invasion of 1940 put an end to all that. The Stirlings escaped from Bordeaux and arrived as refugees in Torquay. Margaret managed to get them a flat in Dolphin Square so that when the air raids started in earnest we all found ourselves huddled together in the air raid shelter in the basement. It wasn't a huddle I minded at all as Pamela was an exceedingly attractive girl with a charming French accent. Unfortunately my Home Guard duties didn't allow me to cuddle up in the shelter as often as I would have liked and then I departed for Oxford.

"Heil Hitler" had an excellent leading role for Pamela and a good mother's role for her mother. Apart from being able to provide a young cast, Oxford was also able to provide a bomb-free place to rehearse in. As soon as I got Margaret's letter I went to Reggie Barr for help and, by the end of November, Edward Stirling came to Oxford to audition a cast. We used Reggie's rooms in the Chapel tower, the young hopefuls making uneasy conversation in the sitting room while Stirling conducted his interviews in the bedroom. My ambition to play the romantic lead opposite Pamela was dashed when the part went to Gordon Davies from Christ Church. The other juvenile lead went to Derek Morphett and I had to be content with a light comedy role as the hero's rather nasty Nazi friend called Steglitz. It was all arranged that we would go into full rehearsal after Christmas aiming for an Easter opening. The fact that the story was considered strong stuff was due to an extraordinary Government ruling before the war prohibiting the making of disparaging remarks about foreign heads of state. It was only in such hot beds of subversion as the Unity Theatre or Martin Blake's flat that Hitler and company could be called the names they deserved.

This was a Trinity/Christ Church production and the same team was due to perform in "Othello" next February. Reggie was to produce and play the lead, Derek Morphett was cast as Cassio and John Eyre from Christ Church was to play Roderigo. John was a passionate admirer of John Gielgud and could be seen striding up and down the Broad Walk imitating the voice and gait of the master. I wondered if he would take offence at the wicked send-up that Michael Flanders had done of Gielgud's Hamlet which could easily have been a take-off of John. Michael was to play Brabantio and I was happy to be given the part of a messenger and general back stage dogsbody.

The term was coming to an end when Reggie asked me if we could have a confidential talk. I went to his room expecting to be told that I wasn't wanted for Othello after all or some such disappointment. To my surprise he was acting for his room mate MacPherson who had run into financial difficulty and couldn't pay his battels. He had been told that unless he paid his bills he would be requested to remain at home for the next term, in other words rusticated. Could I lend him twenty pounds? My father, who paid all my fees and general costs had also given me an allowance of forty pounds a year throughout my school life and had continued with it when I went up to Trinity but at that time twenty pounds was a huge sum.

"I can guarantee that he'll pay you back at the beginning of next term," Reggie said, "and you can have his collection of gramophone records as security."

He showed me what I might inherit if MacPherson failed to pay. Under the window overlooking the front quad were piles of 78s. There must have been at least two hundred of them. No wonder he hadn't any money left. I duly wrote a cheque, hoping secretly that I might acquire his wonderful record collection.

The cause of MacPherson's predicament was a falling out with his father. Most of us had an account with Blackwell's bookshop which our parents underwrote. Unfortunately young MacPherson, having expended all his cash on records and other things, had found that he could buy books on account at Blackwell's and take them across the road to sell for cash at Parker's which dealt in second hand books. What he didn't know was that Blackwell's and Parker's were the same firm. Once Basil B. had been told of these transactions he had telephoned MacPherson senior whose wrath descended upon the son in no uncertain terms. Hence his current problem. Having helped to rescue him from his predicament I packed my bags for home.

The Oxford term is only eight weeks. In the middle of October I had left the ravages of the London blitz to enter the peaceful atmosphere of Trinity College with very tentative thoughts for the future and seemingly unrealisable ambitions. By the middle of December I had had my winning short story published in the Cherwell, acquired an excellent set of friends, been cast in a forthcoming production by Edward Stirling and in Othello by Reggie Barr and had Nevill Coghill as my tutor. Christmas was coming and I looked forward eagerly to 1941.

CHAPTER FIVE

Margaret had escaped from London for a weekend during the term and we had laid our plans for Christmas. My sister Annabel had produced her baby, Fionna, with remarkable lack of judgement on the weekend that Hitler had decided to switch his blitz to central London. One of my first evening duties in September had been to take Fionna in her carry cot down to the shelter. Annabel's husband, Terence, worked in the Bank of England and had managed to find a country cottage where Annabel and Fionna would be reasonably safe until Margaret and I could escort them up to our family home in the Isle of Mull. We decided to break the journey in Glasgow because we found that Jack Hulbert and Cicely Courtneidge with most of the Hulbert family were appearing at the King's Theatre in a cobbled up revue called "The Hulbert Follies".

The show was like a library of famous routines. Songs and sketches which I had only heard on gramophone records leapt into life in live reproduction. "Double Damask", "Laughing Gas", "The Schoolmaster and the Boy","The Ever Open Door", and "Loving You", were interspersed with "The Dowager Fairy Queen" and "The South Is The Place For Me" making an anthology of almost twenty years of comedy. Added in were some new numbers that had been bought for the new show,"Riding High","Room 504", and the rousing "Let's Have Another One" which closed the first half and opened the second. It was a thoroughly entertaining mish-mash designed to make people laugh and forget the war for a while, which seemed an excellent reason for stopping over in Glasgow to renew old acquaintance.

Margaret said that she felt like a deserter leaving London. As the nights had grown longer, the air raid sirens had sounded earlier each evening although the intensity of the raids had lessened after the initial onslaught of September and October. Nevertheless there was a feeling of relief once we had bundled ourselves into the crowded night train from Euston, Annabel plus baby Fionna, Margaret with our beloved spaniels Romeo and Flush and me. For Romeo especially it must have been a blessing because, in spite of his impeccable pedigree, he was hopelessly gun shy. Even a Christmas cracker would send him cringing off into hiding under Margaret's bed, so one can only imagine what it must have been like for the poor creature in our top floor flat in Dolphin Square. Amazingly he never made a mess although it must have been an enormous effort because, as soon as he was taken out into the street after the All Clear, he would produce a flood that made passers by stop in amazement. In his tiny doggy way, Romeo was one of the unsung heroes of the blitz. Flush, being Annabel's dog, had escaped much of the blitz by accompanying her to the country.

We had booked rooms in the Beresford Hotel in Sauchiehall Street. It was a modern art-deco edifice built to accomodate the expected influx of visitors for the Empire Exhibition held in Belahouston Park in 1938. It stuck out like a rude gesture in the grim stateliness of the Victorian streetscape with its two yellow brick columns of bow windows extending up the full ten stories on either side of the theatre-like entrance. In comparison with the more staid and expensive station hotels like the Central, St Enoch's and Queen Street, it was in the category of London's Regent or Strand Palaces. At 10/6 for bed and breakfast it was good value for money.

Staggering into the garishly lit foyer after a twelve hour crawl from London was like being transported to another planet. Glasgow, for some reason had not yet been bombed and seemed to have plenty of everything. There were eggs for breakfast, rashers of real bacon, pats of butter and liberal helpings of lamb for dinner. Surrendering our one day temporary ration cards seemed almost superfluous. Every evening the big lounge was packed with happy people being entertained by George Elrick

Left: *The Beresford (now Baird Hall 1994)*

Below: *All that's left of the Beresford 1994*

King's Theatre Glasgow
The Stage door was to the right of the arched portico.

Cynthia

and his Band -"When you're smiling, when you're smiling, the whole world smiles with you" - and coming from the austerity of battered London it did indeed seem to smile.

The King's Theatre in Bath Street was only one block away. It was built of red sandstone, as is much of Glasgow, in that prolific period of theatre building just after the turn of the century. It was decorated with gilt mirrors and red plush in the manner that James Agate believed all theatres ought to be, having a slightly raffish air of guilty splendour. We took our seats in the Dress Circle and the house lights dimmed. The opening number represented a contrast between the old and the new in dance styles, a decorous waltz by half the chorus countered by

CARELESS TALK COSTS LIVES

a swing version by the other half. It was opened by a single dancer leaping onto the stage to bring the dancers to life with her wand. I thought that she was the prettiest creature I had ever seen and managed to identify her as Cynthia Clifford. I announced that I was going to ask her to meet me. I'm not sure whether my sudden transformation into a stage door Johnny was attributed to my first term at Trinity but it certainly surprised my sisters. The next day I delivered my carefully written letter to the Stage Door. After the show that evening I waited in anxious anticipation to see if anyone would appear. There was an agonizing twenty minutes and then a small figure in a fur coat came into the dim blue light. "Are you John?" She was holding my note. "I'm Cynthia." We walked together back to the Beresford.

One of the advantages of the theatre in wartime was that the shows started early so that it was possible to go to a restaurant at a reasonable hour after the show. In Glasgow the show had started at 6.30 so it was only just after nine o'clock that we wended our way through the black-out curtains into the hotel foyer and I saw Cynthia for the first time off stage. She was far prettier with a mass of wavy dark hair framing a heart shaped face with two huge blue eyes. We deposited our coats in the cloak-room and went into the lounge where the band was blaring and Margaret and Annabel had bagged a table so that they could have a look at what I had got before I took her off to dinner. As we entered the dining room I was flattered at the silence that fell at each table as we passed. Most of the other diners seemed to be in uniform, several Canadians, and some Navy and Air Force officers. Fortunately Cynthia was a chatterer so I didn't have time to be awkward and by the time I had walked her back to her digs which were not far away, I was besotted. My sisters recognised the symptoms and it was decided that we would return South after Christmas via Edinburgh where the show would be. Anything to prevent me from pining away.

In the meantime, getting to Mull had become like a journey to a foreign land. The whole of the West of Scotland was a prohibited area because almost every sea loch or inlet from the Firth of Clyde to the Kyle of Lochalsh was either some form of naval base or a convoy collecting centre. To get to the area it was necessary to prove a legitimate reason to go there, such as bona fide residence, and to be issued with a special green identity card with one's photograph on it like a small passport. The need for all this security became clear when we pulled into Oban station. The town was swarming with the navy blue uniforms of the Royal Australian Air Force who were flying Sunderland and Catalina flying boats from Oban Bay on long range anti-submarine patrols over the Atlantic. Most of the hotels had been commandeered and only the comparatively humble King's Arms, half way between the station and the north pier offered hospitality. Fortunately the small corps of street porters were too old for military service and were available to take our luggage to the boat.

The little Lochinvar was tied up at the North Pier but, before boarding, we had to go through a check point to have our passes stamped. When we cleared the bay and slid out past Dunolly Castle into the Firth of Lorne we found ourselves moving through a mass of merchant ships of all shapes and sizes waiting to sail to America. A flotilla of destroyers or corvettes lay at anchor and further out we saw what looked like the larger outline of a cruiser. We were duly impressed and felt very important as we sailed past Lismore Lighthouse and Duart Castle to pause in Craignure Bay where we had to jump down into the ferry to take us ashore. Although it was early afternoon, it was beginning to get dark as we climbed into Neil MacInnes's old car to rattle along the cart track that passed for a road through the Glen to the Ross of Mull and home.

Although we had been away for almost a year, we had left the keys with Chrissie MacFadyen, who lived in a nearby croft across the peat moss. She had kept the place dusted and greeted us with a blazing peat fire in the drawing room. Annabel tended to our old Ford 10 De Luxe of 1936 vintage which had been wrapped up in the garage and, miraculously, old Florrie started with only a few minor explosions. Even more miraculously our electric light plant - a 1/4 h.p. Kohler - sprung into life with minimal cranking. It was one of those domestic wonders that started when the first light was switched on and switched itself off when the last light was turned out. My father had convinced himself and us that it was a highly expensive operation that used four gallons of petrol a night. The sound of the engine running at night while we read in bed had so worried him that, in the interest of peace, we all provided ourselves with bedside oil lamps and torches. The last time my father had been home was before the Munich crisis, but his four gallons a night illusion had a fortunate result. Annabel had been home at the time when war was declared and had to fill in a form to get a petrol ration to run the plant. In all innocence she

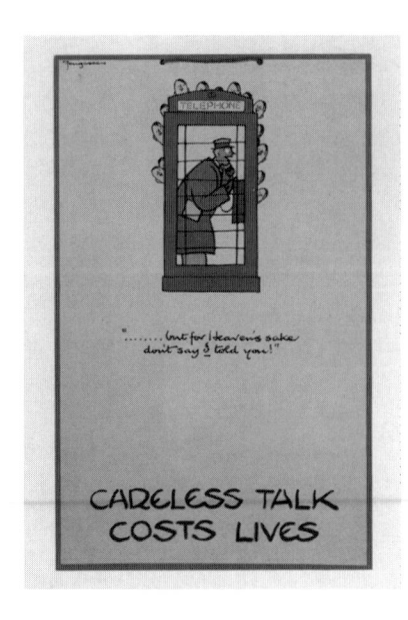

The Lochinvar – how we went to Mull and back

entered my father's figures with the result that two 44-gallon drums of petrol awaited our arrival. We soon discovered that the Kohler ran for at least four hours on less than a gallon of petrol so we were able to run the car as well.

It was a cosy Christmas. There was no shortage of meat as Willie Campbell was the local butcher and even the bureaucrats who supervised the rationing had not devised a way of killing half a sheep. Everyone had hens so there were plenty of eggs and the MacFadyens had a family cow which kept us well provided with milk and cream and fresh home-made butter. But the sort of rationed goods that had to be imported like tea, sugar, and mainland flour had to rely on the ancient ship "Dunara Castle" to make its voyage up the coast from Glasgow every ten days, calling at the island ports on the way. On one occasion, due to the presence of enemy submarines lurking off the coast, she failed to arrive and everyone was reduced to mouldy bread, scones made with the last of the flour and a small store of bramble jelly. It was discovered then that stinging nettles taste like spinach. However Johnnie Cameron, who ran the village shop and post office in Fionnphort half a mile away managed to supply us with sufficient sweets and chocolate to make a cheerful Christmas.

But Oxford was calling and Margaret, who had no need to do so, wanted to get back to London. She was experiencing an emotion that became familiar to front line soldiers that, although it was nice to be out of shell range, life out of the line somehow lacked reality. She also felt a mulish determination not to allow the enemy to drive her out. So, having greeted the New Year, we headed South via Edinburgh.

We stayed in some splendour at the Caledonian Hotel. Jack Hulbert and Cicely Courtneidge occupied a suite on the second floor while we were somewhat higher up the building in the lower price range. The show was playing at the King's Theatre up the Lothian Road and Cynthia was in digs nearby. Then we ran into a slight financial problem. For some reason we found we couldn't pay the hotel bill by cheque so we had to arrange to get cash from our bank. Like most people connected with India we banked with Grindlay's, whose only U.K. office was in London in 55 Parliament Street opposite the Cenotaph. Margaret wrote to get cash sent, but until it arrived we were forced to extend our stay as we didn't dare ask for the bill. Naturally this suited me down to the ground as it meant I could continue to squire Cynthia round the town.

The smart place to dine in Edinburgh was the De Guise room in the Caledonian Hotel. Decked out in Second Empire decor with lots of mirrors and candelabra, it had a small dance floor and a live band. Taking Cynthia there was the most sophisticated and expensive thing I had ever done. I had assumed that I would be able to sign the bill with my room number as I had done at the Beresford. But no, the De Guise room was separate and cash was required. To my embarassment I had to rely on Cynthia's aid to pay the bill to the exact penny. There wasn't even enough to tip the waiter. The clientele was largely noisy parties of naval officers letting off steam after a spell at sea. At the table next to ours one of the diners had subsided onto the floor with a hunting horn which he blew whenever he wanted another drink. A group of army officers was loudly discussing their impending departure from Leith and altogether the posters warning us that "Careless Talk Costs Lives" were being happily ignored. To balance the equation, a rather quieter table of heavily bandaged RAF officers from a nearby hospital served to remind us that there really was a war on. But, except for the inconvenience of the black-out, Edinburgh like Glasgow seemed to be irritatingly peaceful so, as soon as our money arrived, we left for London. My parting from Cynthia was mollified by the impending arrival of "The Hulbert Follies" in Oxford in February. We piled into our crowded train at Waverley Station for the long haul South.

CHAPTER SIX

Hilary term started sadly with the news that A.G. MacDonnell had died. His flat was across the Broad over Castell's the tailors and he was a familiar figure looking like everyone's idea of a literary giant complete with cape and homberg. James Agate described him as a "paradoxical dandy" with his red carnation smiling and his glasses frowning. His book "England Their England" will probably stand as his lasting memorial with his description of the village cricket match being one of the great pieces of comic writing. It seemed such a short time since we had heard his witty speech at the Oxford Union in the debate on the theatre and, although I had only managed to exchange a few polite words with him at the Friends of the OUDS reception, it was impossible not to feel a personal sadness at his loss. I am sure that, if he had lived, he would have been pleased to see signs of a theatrical revival in Oxford.

The first symptom was an excellent production of "Hedda Gabler" at the Playhouse. Julian d'Albie had roped in James Agate to help with the production. His availability was, in part, due to the presence of John Byron in the cast who had obtained rooms in Oxford for Agate to make his escape from the London bombing for a while. To judge by his diary, Agate found the experience of actually helping to create a performance instead of just criticising it very exciting, and certainly he helped to provide a most stimulating evening of theatre. Julian d'Albie played Judge Brack, John Byron Eilert Lovborg, Rosalie Crutchley Mrs Elvsted and Pamela Brown Hedda. Agate discovered that having to cast a play from an existing list of actors meant that many of them were obliged to play against

Pamela Brown in Hedda Gabler. Oxford Playhouse 1941

their personalities. It was precisely this necessity that made the British repertory system, for all its faults, such an excellent training ground for the profession. For example he "got rid of much of d'Albie's charm, which is too genial, and got him to replace it by the cold suavity of your man of the world" and persuaded "handsome John Byron not to look at his first entry as though he had just made a century in the Varsity match". I must say that I was surprised at John Byron's performance as I had previously only seen him as a musical comedy song and dance man. Perhaps that would explain his exuberant first entry. Agate also had the salutory experience of attending the dress rehearsal "which was a shambles" and consoled himself by looking at the "lovely dresses Tony Holland has designed". However it was all right on the night as Ivor Brown wrote in "The Observer",

"At Oxford there has not, I believe, been a new play for a year or so, and the business, as I saw is grand. Also the quality of the acting. This is a first rate company which ought not to be spending all its time on the repertory treadmill. It's Hedda Gabler was an adventure, if not a novelty, and it was given the public's eager support. Were I a dramatist I should be very happy to have my leading feminine part 'created' by Miss Pamela Brown, whose Hedda was much spoken of - and rightly so. Even putting Ibsen on stage (during a snowstorm) failed to deter the swarmers at the box office."

It was this review together with Agate's own in the Sunday Times, that launched Pamela Brown on the road to stardom, as in the film "I Know Where I'm Going" in which she starred with Roger Livesey and Deborah Kerr and which, coincidentally, was shot in Mull. It set a notable standard for the coming term as the Cherwell enthusiastically commented in its Oxford Notebook.

"The most exciting feature of a not particularly eventful week was, to many of us at least, the astounding success of the Oxford Repertory Players' production of Hedda

Gabler. Leslie French attempted to run a series of "better" plays at the same theatre last summer, but these were so poorly supported, in spite of the producer's inimitable exhortations nightly from the stage, that last term the company felt reluctantly compelled to resort to commonplace contemporary farces in an endeavour to satisfy the popular taste. This plan coincided with the invasion of the evacuees, and a public that was used to the London theatre, finding an unusually poor season of variety at the New Theatre, filled the Playhouse night after night."

"It was a wonderfully brave venture to depart, even for a week, from a venture that had resulted in such unbroken success. Mr Agate was, one imagines, largely responsible for this, but the whole cast was yearning for parts that would offer them some scope. The first signs of the public's reaction were alarming; many first-night regulars cancelled their weekly bookings; but Mr Agate's letter to Oxford Playgoers found its way to the darkest corners of the University, and the "House Full" board was displayed more times than one can remember having seen it in recent years. It would have been a sin had there been an empty seat on Saturday night, which was a memorable occasion for those of us who were lucky enough to have booked early in the week. It is perhaps significant that the house was sold out for the first night of Laburnum Grove by early Monday afternoon. Fanatical visions come to mind of Oxford supporting first-class plays in the face of the terrible rivalry of the Musical Comedy; one may hope that when the stars begin to roll up in George Street the Oxford Playgoer will sacrifice one flick a week to enable the Repertory Company, by his regular support, to satisfy his demands when there is no super-attraction to divert his attention".

The Cherwell's enthusiasm was tempered with considerable cynicism when it came to commenting on our own efforts to get things going.

"Acting enthusiasts within the University are finding it

well-nigh impossible to produce plays, and spend their time leaping hopefully from bough to bough as each one breaks. The exciting proposal of the Trinity and Christ Church Dramatic Societies to perform the successful American thriller "Heil Hitler" at the Playhouse for the first time in this country fell through, not through lack of support in any respect, but simply because no theatre was available. The Clarendon Press Institute, where so many exciting performances have succeeded in over-coming the rival noises of ping-pong in the adjoining hall, is no longer in use, and the Taylorian is hard to come by without fingers in various pies. The Conservative Association have performed something like a miracle in securing it for a week late in the term; they are presenting the Friends of the OUDS in a play which has not yet been decided upon, and at present seems to be hovering between Othello and Traitor's Gate, Morna Stuart's play of Sir Thomas More. The Christ Church Dramatic Society's production of The Ascent of F6 which promised good things, has been abandoned because, so I heard, the Upper Library is being secretly equipped for fire-watching. Some brave spirits in Queen's and the Slade are preparing an unusual modern play "Hosea" which I am looking forward to, having had the elements of the plot inadequately explained to me - though where and when I am not sure,"

Michael Meyer went on to comment on the formation of The New Britain Club and the revival of inter-college sport with "Cuppers" being arranged for rugger and hockey and presumed that soccer would soon follow suit. But in fact the beginning of the term was a miserable one for sport, with snow and slush and freezing temperatures making rugby, hockey, soccer and athletics out of the question until the thaw. Torpids were abandoned because, during the first week of term, ice-bergs were floating down the river and no rowing was possible. It was a bleak start to the year.

However the prognostication that the Stars would roll up in George Street was true. After the pantomime "Babes in the Wood" ended in January, the New Theatre hosted a list of productions that would have tested the competition of any theatre. First came Rex Harrison, Diana Wynyard and Lilli Palmer in "No Time For Comedy", then came Alfred Drayton and Robertson Hare in "Women Aren't Angels", Owen Nares and Peggy Ashcroft in "Rebecca" and Jack Hulbert and Cicely Courtneidge in "The Hulbert Follies". Reggie Barr, who could do a convincing imitation of Robertson Hare, delighted in telling us that he had heard him booming "I don't like the Randolph, it's too pompous." He preferred a more modest establishment near the railway station but for the majority of the visiting stars the Randolph or the Mitre were the places to stay and be seen.

Against this influx of West End stars the Playhouse managed to hold its own, following "Laburnum Grove" with "The Two Mrs Carrolls", "Petticoat Influence", "By Candlelight", "White Cargo", "Family Affairs", John Masefield's "The Witch" and "The Seagull" which John Heath-Stubbs unkindly said looked "more like a pelican".

And the prospects for University drama was not quite as gloomy as the writer of the Oxford Diary in The Cherwell made out.

"Othello" had been decided upon in the previous term and was in full rehearsal. Michael Flanders had not entirely abandoned his production of "The Ascent of F6" in spite of being cast as Brabantio in "Othello" and Antony Hinton was directing "Salome" for the Experimental Theatre Club with Sonia South in the title role, Hallam Fordham as Saint John, Freddie Hurdis Jones as Herod and Molly Spencer as Herodias. This was to be followed in March by Strindberg's "Ghost Sonata", so the ETC was in full swing.

But from a personal point of view I was more interested in the forthcoming performance of "Hosea". This was a morality play written by Sidney Keyes. Sidney was a school friend of Paddy Engelbach's at Tonbridge and Paddy had already been impressed by his prowess as a poet. Soon after he came to Oxford he came under the wing of John Heath-Stubbs who recognised his talent and encouraged his work which was first published in the Cherwell. In fact one of Sidney's poems shared a page of the Cherwell of the 20th February with my article urging us to revive our theatre. It was followed a week later by the first poem to be published by Philip Larkin, "Tired of a Landscape Too Well Known When Young." By the beginning of the Hilary term Paddy was getting a bit worried because Sidney was showing increasing signs of being self-consciously arty.

"Surely you can be a poet without having to dress like one," Paddy said in some exasperation. It was true that, in contrast to our conservative choice of clothes, Sidney had taken to wearing corduroy trousers and jackets with a green shirt and coloured bow ties. But then he *was* at Queen's as someone waspishly pointed out.

However no-one could gainsay the triumphant success of his play. It was a co-production of the Queen's College Dramatic Society and the Slade School of Art which had been evacuated from London and was housed for the duration in the Ashmolean. Basil Taylor played Hosea, Roy Porter, who was no mean poet himself, played the enigmatic Mister X. Diana Yeldham-Taylor designed the set and costumes. It was hailed by the Oxford Magazine, the mouthpiece of the Dons, as "an eminently successful morality - one of the best productions we have seen by amateurs in Oxford" and " a triumphant success". The first performance took place in the Taylorian Institute at 2.30 p.m. on a Wednesday. Not the most auspicious time for a world premiere but it gave me my first look at the hall in which we were later to perform "Othello" and also my first look at the Bandits.

The Bandits were the Oxford University Dance Band and they had been engaged to provide the second half of the show because "Hosea" only ran for just over an hour. It wasn't a bad amateur dance band playing the standard arrangements supplied by Brons.

Every Thursday afternoon the agonised discords of its rehearsals could be heard wafting across Magdalen Street to the Broad and Cornmarket from the first floor of Taphouses Music shop. The band was led by the son of a Durham miner called Frank Dixon whose sartorial idiosyncracy was to wear a single stud in his collarless shirt when he wasn't dressed up in the tuxedo and black tie uniform of the band. The lead trumpeter was Ronnie Wilkinson, who later became a successful playwright himself, with Roger Frisby and John Boothby. Denis Mathew was the pianist. Some years later Denis and I teamed up with Donald Swann to provide the music for the ETC Revue "Oxford Circus" at the Playhouse Theatre, London. But on this occasion I was more interested in the drummer whose chair I envied. Regrettably Alan Lazarus was an excellent drummer whose work can probably still be heard in the BBC archives in a recording they made of "Dark Blues". Their programme was, to say the least, catholic. "Song of India", "Pennsylvania 6-5000", "The Maid's Night Out", "The Wedding of Pocahontas", and "Orpheus in the Underworld" played on a penny whistle. The

Sydney Keyes, aged 20. Regrettably he never made it to 21.

fact that they came on after the interval caused a certain amount of umbrage because the theatre critic of the Cherwell went home after the play and never mentioned their performance. However the Oxford Magazine called it "a cheering entertainment" and Paddy basked in the reflected glory of being a friend of the author. I looked gloomily round the austere inadequacy of the Taylor Institute as a theatre. I reckoned that Reggie Barr was going to have his work cut out to mount a full scale Shakespearean production in a hall designed to be no more than a lecture theatre.

CHAPTER SEVEN

Paddy Engelbach had a problem. His father expected him to get a Blue. Paddy's father was a noted Egyptologist and one of the top echelon of the National Museum in Cairo. Paddy was full of tales of the mysteries of the tombs of the Pharoahs and the inside story of the uncovering of the tomb of Tutenkhamen with its range of unexplained misfortunes for those involved. Paddy enjoyed tales of misfortune. He was a dark, stocky, saturnine young man with a quirky sense of humour. He was reading Modern Languages and seemed to be concentrating on German because he was fascinated by the diabolical minds of the Nazis.

"What sort of people are they who can seriously sit down and invent tortures because the tortures they already have are not painful enough?" he once asked. He was the only person I have ever met who was a genuine agnostic.

"It isn't that I don't believe", he told me, "it's simply that I don't know. You can't commit yourself to something you don't know."

One of the things he didn't know was how he was going to get a blue to please his father.

Fortunately we had among us one Nigel Mathew, a formidable pugilist from his school days at Lancing and the only punch-drunk undergraduate of our year. Nigel persuaded Paddy that the best way to get a Blue was to take up boxing and try to qualify for the University team which was short of members. Nigel himself was pretty sure of his place in the team and so was another Trinity man of our year, Peter Balmer. So Paddy, being a pragmatist, became a boxer. He also took up Judo. I hoped that his boxing was better that his Judo because the only time he tried to show me some clever hold or other he gave a heave and fell flat on his back while I remained standing. "I don't think I got that quite right," was probably the understatement of the term. Nevertheless Paddy was tough, courageous and determined and Nigel reckoned he could make it.

At the beginning of 1941, boxing was as good a way as any of trying to keep warm. That first week of term was miserable with the snow and slush making the parade to the bath house an exercise in determination. The reward was to be able to luxuriate in a bath of boiling hot water for as long as the next person would let you. The baths were in cubicles with only a curtain across the door so that anyone who was considered to be hogging it could be unceremoniously dispossessed. Then it was a dash for the JCR in the hope of getting near the fire. It was a spartan existence, a veritable winter of discontent. It made the petty irritations of the war seem even less bearable.

A Government drive to collect scrap iron for the war effort had resulted in the removal of a lot of the railings from parks and gardens, ostensibly to be melted down to make munitions or tanks or something. It was probably necessary but in the cold and miserable conditions it was greeted with the sort of reaction of the anonymous writer in the Oxford Magazine who sent in "A Cry from a Grass Plot in Front of the Botanical Gardens."

"I gave my railings to the nation
To save our people from the Hun.
Our people, in appreciation,
And in a spirit of good fun,
Return, as gratitudes donation,
Cigarette cartons by the ton.
For crass insensate desecration
Our British public takes the bun."

Huddled figures filled the unheated libraries wrapped up for warmth. Balaclavas in the Bodleian. The undergraduate uniform of sports jacket and flannels was augmented by V-necked cable stitched sweater or even polo necks. Even I buttoned up my overcoat and wrapped my scarf round my ears.

Affectation surrendered to necessity. Reggie Barr sensibly made his room the centre for rehearsals so that he remained warm while we thawed under his direction. It must have pretty dreary for his room mate MacPherson being excluded from his share of the sitting room with its cosy fire. Nor presumably could he enjoy playing his huge collection of gramophone records which he had redeemed from my clutches at the beginning of term by repaying his loan.

But apart from just keeping warm, we had other more serious concerns.

When the call-up age was reduced to 18 in March 41, it became necessary to obtain an exemption to continue at University. This was granted on condition that you enrolled for training in the University Senior Training Corps or its Naval or Air Force equivalent. For example, Vernon St John and Paddy Engelbach joined the University Air Squadron, and David Marsh and I clattered with most of the others in our battle-dress, boots and gaiters to parade on the Broad Walk by Christ Church meadows.

The STC was run by the Brigade of Guards and so we were subjected to all the routine badinage of that splendid organisation. Yells from the RSM echoed over the meadows as we marched and counter-marched up and down the Broad Walk, or charged with fixed bayonets at the straw filled dummies lined up on the grass outside Merton.

"Come on, Sir, show a bit of aggression, you don't want them to die laughing."

We stripped off our buttoned up tunics for the more energetic exercises revealing a most unsoldierlike array of assorted shirts, for our uniforms, like our military skills, were mostly superficial. We took it in turns to lead sections in mock attacks across the meadows, trying to avoid the cowpats as we tumbled to the ground and pretended to engage some distant enemy.

Down, crawl, observe, fire. Some of us attracted the personal scorn of our mentors.

"Mister Lord Fitzmaurice Sir!" rang out on one occasion. It was a form of address designed to put anyone in his place,

The Broad Walk where the Senior Training Corps paraded.

Christ Church meadows. The cowpats are still there -so are the cows.

The area in front of Merton College where the OUSTC did bayonet drill.

The Broad Walk in Christ Church meadow. Magdalen College steeple in the distance.

especially as the unfortunate young man had only recently crashed his car. And so it went on, punctuating our lives and keeping us constantly reminded that we were only undergraduates on sufferance. Paddy thought I was mad.

"Why don't you join the RAF," he kept nagging, "and drive to war in comfort and sleep in a decent billet each night."

I thought of the Heinkel lying on top of the jewellers outside Victoria Station and the Spitfire I had seen spiralling down over Eaton Square.

"Because I'm a natural groundling," I said, "and I can hardly drive a car let alone one of those noisy machines and if anything goes wrong I can't fall out of my boots."

Our interest in matters military seemed to have centred more on the possibilities of physical discomfort than in any thoughts of danger. But mostly we preferred not to think of that sort of future at all.

All of us had been in our school OTCs, or Junior Training Corps as they later became, and had passed the Certificate "A" examination which, in the previous Great War, had been deemed sufficient to enable a young man of 18 to be given an immediate commission as a Second Lieutenant to lead a platoon over the top in the Flanders mud bath. Membership of the Senior Training Corps enabled you to pass the Certificate "B" examination which meant that, on being called up, you only did an abbreviated recruits course before going on to an OCTU - Officer Cadet Training Unit.

The idea of a democratic army in which everyone was promoted through the ranks had to be observed however superficially. But it was made very clear that attending these parades and passing the army exam was far more important than anything you might do either academically or on the sporting field. If you failed to attend the parades your deferment from the call-up could be speedily cancelled. Added to this was the necessity to volunteer. It wasn't enough to sit back and let events take their course. Even this was not left to chance. One day the STC notice board listed all the newest members to parade at 1430 hours "to volunteer for the army."

We were marched in threes to a Drill Hall somewhere

down the back of St Ebbe's for our induction. Here we wandered about naked except for our socks to pee into test tubes and have our balls held while we coughed. The theory that two doctors looked into each ear and, if they couldn't see each other you were in, might well have applied. At the end of it all we signed a form, received 2/6 pay plus 2/6 ration allowance - the modern equivalent of the King's shilling - and we were in. For some reason which only the War Office might explain we were enrolled in the Royal Fusiliers, not, as might be expected, the local Oxfordshire and Buckinghamshire Light Infantry. They say you never forget your army number and 6477204 is the one that sheer fright has imprinted on my brain. As we marched back to be formally dismissed, we passed the platoon of Signals Officer Cadets, wearing commoners gowns over their uniforms, being marched off to a lecture on electronics. At least we could get to our tutorials and lectures in our own time once we were out of uniform.

After being officially enrolled in H.M. Forces, we found ourselves the object of attention of the recruiting officers of various regiments. It was made pretty clear that Oxford men were expected to go into the Guards or the Greenjackets unless they could find a good excuse to go elsewhere. Nevil Macready's father was a Gunner General as had been his father before him so clearly Nevil opted for the same. David Marsh chose the Welsh Guards but I'm not sure why, he may have just fancied the badge. Having been stuck out in India with my parents when the war started, I nearly became a Gurkha except for the fact that my call-up papers for that elite outfit arrived after I had sailed for Britain. However I found that the Rifle Brigade and the King's Royal Rifle Corps were sister regiments and had the advantage of having black buttons which didn't have to be polished. As a bonus they were something called Motor Battalions which seemed to imply the possibility of less walking, so for those quite ignoble reasons, when interviewed by their very gentlemanly team of Officers, I opted for them. Strangely it never occurred to me to opt for my home county regiment the Argyll and Sutherland Highlanders nor even for the Gloucesters who had nurtured my school training corps. I suppose that having been in the London Home Guard I regarded myself a Londoner and to join a cockney regiment seemed logical. Anyway the result of all this military activity was that my call-up was deferred for a year and I could get on with my life with a clear conscience.

CHAPTER EIGHT

The Hulbert Follies arrived at the New Theatre in February. Nevil, Paddy, David and I went to the Monday opening night and round to the stage door after the show. Cynthia introduced us to the rest of the girls and, as a polite formality I introduced myself to the Stage Director Laurence Green and was ushered in to see Cicely Courtneidge and Jack Hulbert. After all the polite inquiries about Margaret and Annabel, Cicely let us away to attend to the main business of the evening.

Nevil had identified a pretty honey blond in the chorus as Renna Caste and Paddy was greatly taken with a vivacious blonde called Iris Tully. David contented himself with thinking about Deanna Durbin. Dates were arranged and the inevitable invitation to tea.

We duly assembled in Room 13 to indulge ourselves in the usual array of buttered toast and honey, fruit cake and, of course, a Fullers Walnut cake, but only Cynthia turned up as the others had been called to some extra rehearsal. So Cynthia happily held court while my room became a centre of attention. Suddenly everyone seemed to have an urgent reason to visit. Vernon had an urgent message for Paddy about the Air Squadron, Reggie Barr felt the need to discuss a rehearsal for "Othello", and the David's, Humphreys and Aiers pottered in for no reason at all. So the introduction of Cynthia into Trinity can be deemed to have been a success. Less successful was my personal pursuit.

The trouble was that Cynthia was a flirtatious nineteen year old who had been in show business since she was in her early teens and, I'm sure, thought that I was just a silly boy. She had been one of the Ovaltinis on the Radio Luxemburg commercial radio and had spent the year before she joined the Hulberts as a dancer in the chorus of the Windmill Theatre.

The Windmill was the last survivor of the pre-war craze for non-stop revue in London. It was a ploy to try to compete with the cinema and meant that from about ten in the morning till midnight you could go into the theatre at any time and sit through the show until the part you had already seen came on and then you could leave, just like the cinema. Hence the well-known catch phrase, "This is where we came in." When the Government closed the theatres at the beginning of the war, and later when most of them closed because of the blitz, Vivian van Damm, who owned the Windmill, refused to do so and it became the theatre's proud boast that "We never closed."

The format was a mixture of revue sketches, comedy, glamour and nudity. It was a breeding ground for a string of comedians like Peter Sellers, Jimmy Edwards, Derek Roy, Benny Hill, Frankie Howerd, and Spike Milligan. It also featured two well-drilled dancing choruses, working alternate shows, but it must be admitted that it was the nudes that attracted the audience. The laws of stage nudity were strict. Posing in the nude was allowed on the pretext that it was Art, but if the girl moved a muscle it was pornography. So the Windmill nudes used to stand in dramatic poses in tableaux purporting to represent such noble themes as Liberty, the Spirit of Art, Venus arising from the ocean, and probably Equality and Fraternity, while the audience scrambled for each front seat as it became vacant. Some hardy souls were known to have sat the show round several times as they advanced their positions forward. Cynthia was careful to ensure that she was identified as a dancer but nevertheless the fact that she had been a "Windmill Girl" had a certain cachet that presented me with challenging implications. The trouble was that I terribly wanted to kiss her.

I had never kissed a girl in my life but, of course, I had seen it done many times on the screen so I knew more or less how to go about it. The trouble was that the girls on the screen always seemed to be expecting it whereas Cynthia obviously wasn't. Each day, as I took her back to her digs in Walton Street after the show, I would think of how to line her up for the fateful moment, but she would prattle on happily and be up the steps and in the front door before I could get my hands out of my pockets. When I got back to college I would have to face up to the knowing looks of Paddy or David or Nevil who would know that I hadn't made it. The fact that they were having no more success with their girls never occurred to me.

Things were getting desperate. Saturday was approaching and soon the show would be off to goodness knows where and here was I the tragic figure of unrequited love. Determination overcame my fear.

As we reached her doorstep I said firmly, "Hang on." She paused and turned. I took her by the shoulders and lunged forward for my practised kiss. Unfortunately she was standing on the step and I was at ground level and somehow or other I only managed to catch her a glancing pout on the cheek. She giggled and I thought I wanted to die.

"You are silly," she said, stepping down to my level and I don't remember walking back to college at all.

Cynthia's visit to Oxford had long term repercussions on our family fortunes. When she had come to my room she had seen my snare drum parked in the corner and had introduced me to Len Hunt who was touring as percussionist with the show. Len was one of the leading percussionists in the business and I think he was amused at an Oxford undergraduate being so keen. He gave me several valuable lessons culminating with an invitation to sit with him in the orchestra pit for the Saturday show. In those days all shows ended with the playing of the National Anthem and, to my delight, Len handed me the sticks to strike the roll for it. After the anthem came the routine march out, consisting of a short selection of numbers from the show while the audience left. I think that the pat on the back from Len and the approving nod from Bob Probst, who was the musical director, as we struck the final chord was one of my happiest moments.

My sister Margaret came up from London for a couple of nights to see the show and was introduced to Len. He took her solemnly aside.

"You want to watch that brother of yours." he said.
"You mean about Cynthia? That's just puppy love."
"No, no, he wants to be a professional drummer. You mustn't encourage him, he's too good, it's too easy for him, he'll turn into a spiv."

When I heard this I was elated. He couldn't have paid me a greater compliment, and it established a friendship which was to have lasting consequences.

By the end of the Oxford run we had found that the show was to have a week's break after playing Morecambe in April so Paddy, Nevil and I arranged to go up to Mull for a couple of weeks during the Easter vacation and take Cynthia and the other two girls with us. So ended a happy week.

The local reviews of the Hulbert Follies provided an interesting contrast. The Oxford Mail headed its review "A Fine Tonic" and said "it must be a long time since an Oxford audience has given so complete a demonstration of its goodwill towards the play as that which Jack Hulbert, Cicely Courtneidge and Claude Hulbert received at the New Theatre last night." It went on to single out Jack singing "The flies crawled up the window", Cicely in "The South is the place for me" and " The dowager fairy queen", Claude as "Drake" and as Arthur Bloom in "The ever-open door," and gave special mention to Pamela-Rosemary, the Hulbert's daughter, Betty Martin, Henry Thompson, Eunice Crowther and Iris Tully. It was summed up as "a most enjoyable evening."

The Oxford Magazine agreed, praising the show, especially the "Ballet Egyptien" which it rightly said wouldn't sound funny if you described it! Nevertheless it put its foot in it by saying that "the Folly Girls suffered a little from first night trouble, but once they found the show was going well they brightened up a lot and the audience came to accept them for what they were, cheerful learners with quite their fair share of budding talent." But this didn't greatly please the hand-picked Hulbert chorus line, most of whom had worked together since the triumphant opening of "Under Your Hat" in 1938 and were judged within the profession to be the best drilled troupe in the country.

However Basil Webb, writing in the Cherwell, attacked

the show savagely. He described a short sketch about the Queen visiting a bombed-out cockney couple as being the last refuge of a distracted wartime producer and "too bad to be either effective or funny." He hated Claude Hulbert as Drake - a song and dance routine which frequently stopped the show - and said that there was "a curious amateurishness about the whole show. It was redolent throughout of a Pierrot on the beach." Which, as the Oxford Magazine pointed out, was exactly what it was meant to be, even to the Pierrot costumes worn by the cast. But Basil Webb was reflecting the undergraduate desire to be patronisingly different. He wanted "new numbers" (there were in fact several including "Riding High", "I Didn't Know What Time It Was", and "Room 504" which became a top ten hit). "We want new sketches with point and snap to them and we want some new stars", which was difficult with a show featuring the biggest stars of the day in their classic sketches and routines. All of this was not of any great moment except it appeared in the issue after my article on reviving University theatre so my connection with the magazine made the company think that I might be something of a Quisling. Cicely Courtneidge didn't appreciate being called "amateurish", but Jack, as a Cambridge man, dismissed it as just what one would expect from Oxford.

After the departure of the Hulberts, life settled down into the routine that became more or less standard for the next couple of terms. Nevil's rooms in St John's became our social centre where we would foregather at the start of the evening before heading off for the Flam or a theatre or cinema. We were a pretty hearty lot and fairly noisy. If the gramophone wasn't blaring, we would sing bawdy songs or shout jokes or anecdotes, so it was inevitable that someone should suggest that we collect the words of the songs and compile an Oxford Book of Dirty Ditties. Paddy Engelbach and David Humphreys became the custodians of our researches and during the year had compiled a fairly comprehensive collection; Andrew Clair, which we found became Anthony in Cambridge, Little Angeline, The Good Ship Venus, The Derby Ram, A Sailor Told Me, If I Were A Marrying Girl, and so on. Nevil swore that he had met a parson in the bar of the Randolph who said he knew a hundred and eight verses of the Ball of Kirriemuir. This would have delighted Ian Mollison who made rather a speciality of it. He also had a little song with which he used to regale us about an old farmer who lived on a rock and which ended with a triumphant shout of "it's bullshit I'm sure!"

This was the first time I had heard the word which would dominate much of my future army service. Ian's triumphant shout frequently echoed round the Chapel quad. There were recitations too. "It nearly broke the family's heart when Lady Jane became a tart", was attributed to A.P. Herbert while an epic called "Lady Clodagh Stanley" was supposed to be read to a man without his trousers who had to pay a forfeit if it gave him an erection. Philip Larkin, who was on the next staircase to Nevil's where he uneasily shared a sitting room with Eddie Stewart, used to join us for the jazz and was enthusiastic about the vigour and drive of the rhyming verses which, he rightly claimed, were the stuff of genuine uninhibited folk song. And good rousing tunes they had too. We tried to enlist Reggie Barr to write them down but he was too busy with the threat of exams and preparations for "Othello". So the words were assiduously written down by Paddy and David in a schoolroom note book and taken off when they went into the RAF and never seen again.

Apart from singing lustily or lustfully about them, girls didn't play a great part in our lives. Esmund Seal, who lived in digs, excited our admiration by sleeping with a sexy girl he called his "bed woman" who drove a milk delivery van. He seemed a knowledgeable sort of chap at the time with his descriptions of the different positions they had tried - "we couldn't move and I got cramp but it was new" - and he introduced us to the amazing, if apocryphal, Colonel Waterhouse. The good Colonel, so we were assured, had been crossed in love and thereafter travelled the world in pursuit of sexual gratification. After many presumably exhausting years, he had produced a treatise on his experiences. In order of excellence he listed his most exciting sexual encounters as being first with a water melon, secondly a cow, and thirdly, buggering a Spanish woman. Who he was or where he had lodged his famous treatise was never explained but it appealed to our inquiring minds. It would have made an interesting appendix to the Oxford Book of Dirty Ditties.

Our sexual lives were almost entirely empirical and mostly non-existent. Still hope burned eternal and most of us went to a little herbalist's shop in New Inn Hall street and bought a packet of French Letters. The braver and more flamboyant souls ostentatiously carried one in their wallets, more in hope than anything else, while others, perhaps out of frustration, waited till they were in the Gods at the theatre, inflated the wretched thing and floated it down onto the stalls. There were some, though, whose sexual knowledge was greater than could have been gleaned from Van der Velde or the stilted sex talk that accompanied one's departure from school for what was sinisterly called The Big Outside World.

Paddy Engelbach's friend Ian de Hamil was a most sophisticated young man inhabiting a ground floor room on the South side of the quad in New College. There he had surrounded himself with the appurtenances of affluence and affectation. A grand piano was the centre-piece of his room which he had equipped with a Cona coffee percolator, a silver tray with decanters of brandy, dry sherry and port and the necessary ballons and liquer glasses. Cointreau, creme de menthe, and drambuie were discreetly tucked away in the cupboard. After dinner he would entertain his guests by playing Debussy or singing lieder in his light tenor voice while the coffee percolated. Then he would serve it with a dash of rosewater in wafer thin bone china. He liked to change for dinner and affected an embroidered smoking jacket and a long cigarette holder.

But there was nothing effeminate about Ian to judge by his tales of successful seduction. He introduced us to the potential wonders of the chemical pessary, a small pill which, we were assured, produced a contraceptive foam that guaranteed total safety and protection.

"I don't care for those rubber things and dutch caps and devices," he once said, "They interrupt the natural flow of things. I find I can press one of these in with my thumb at the 'moment critique' and it works like a charm."

Later, in the secrecy of my bedroom, I tried balancing an aspirin on the end of my thumb to see how it would work and had to admit that, even if it had stayed there, I would have had no idea where to press it.

At the time, Ian professed to be passionately in love with a young actress called Muriel Pavlow but I'm not sure if he had ever met her. His other passion was a huge Rudge-Whitworth motor cycle. It packed about 1000cc of engine power and Ian's delight was to roar round the Oxfordshire lanes at 100 miles an hour. He took Paddy for a ride on his padded pillion and brought him back pale and sweating but exhilarated. He once gave me a lift from Magdalen Bridge to Carfax which was enough for me. "La Cathedrale Engloutie" always revives memories of New College, lolling against the cushions, drinking coffee, sipping the excellent college port, smoking Balkan Sobranie cigarettes and talking, talking, talking.

This same New College quad also housed another sybaritic inhabitant called Felix Hope-Nicholson. He too affected the long cigarette holder and the Noel Coward dressing gown but, unlike Ian, he seemed to attract the unwelcome attention of the heartier element. Because of the war there was a large static water tank in the centre of the quad and occasionally the cry would go up, "Let's chuck Felix in the water tank."

Off the posse would go intent on seizing the unfortunate young man. Once the cry went up in St John's and off we went with determined tread. By the time we had stumped up the Broad and under the Bridge of Sighs there was a tendancy for some to veer off down the narrow passage-way to the Turf, but a small group reached Felix's room. When our leader had opened his door, we found Felix lying on a chaise longue, naked in his dressing gown, smoking a black Russian cigarette. He must surely have been expecting us.

"Come in dear boys," he cried, "do have a drink. Do you really want to throw me in the water tank, how very tedious. Oh well, if you must —"

By this time our enthusiasm had rather waned, the walk from St John's had diffused the alcohol and I don't think we took up his offer to jump in if it would amuse us. The trouble was that Felix was a nice person and it takes a bit of courage to handle a group of drunken hearties such as we must have seemed to be. There were some who unkindly suggested that he actually enjoyed being man handled. Perhaps so.

Nocturnal pranks punctuated the year aided by the blackout. A group calling itself the Anti-Nobblers League indulged in stealing the brass plates off houses and businesses in order to try to return them in daylight without being caught. It was a strange vice. A lady who lived in the Broad, just along from the Trinity gate had a name which unfortunately could not fail to attract the predatory attentions of the passing drunk. She was called Miss Smallpiece. At least once a term her brass name plate disappeared and the simple message, "Please put it back," was

Lloyd's Bank where the Anti-Nobblers League's attempt to return the brass plate ended in flight.

pinned to her door. The Anti-Nobblers thought she was too easy a target, being more interested in something challenging like the huge brass plate outside Lloyd's Bank on the corner of Cornmarket and the High. It proved to be heavier than expected and after spending the night in St John's it was wrapped in brown paper and carried back down the Cornmarket the next morning. It had been decided that it would not be possible to screw it back into place without being foolhardy so Nevil and Esmund carried it between them and leant it against the big swing door. The weight of the plate pushed the door open and it fell with a loud clang into the marble floored hall. The Anti-Nobblers fled.

The University Mountaineering Club had a reputation for nocturnal daring. Having been denied the recent opportunity to climb the occasional Alp, they practised their craft on the Oxford buildings placing defiant chamber pots on prominent places - no less than six in one night on the Exeter College Chapel - and using their mountain rescue skills to help anyone who had the misfortune to come to grief while climbing into college. They made a notable rescue of a Hertford man who had fallen into the basement area and broken his leg. He was hoisted out and got to bed so that his friends could tell the authorities that he had simply fallen down stairs. Their most notable achievement in 1941 came at the end of the year after the Russians had been invaded and we were getting a series of visits from prominent Communist "heroes". Some senior Russian dignitary was visiting Oxford and the Red Flag was flown in his honour on Carfax. That night, although the tower was locked, the flag disappeared. It was later delivered to the Mayor made up into a smoking jacket with the hammer and sickle on the breast pocket.

Some nocturnal escapades were harmless and occasionally witty. Outside the Exeter Chapel there are two statues of Saints looking suitably contemplative. It took some time before someone noticed that the subject of one of their contemplations was a fanned hand of five aces. Sometimes what seemed funny at the time turned out to be less so in the morning. Trinity's Simon Partridge found himself on the platform at Oxford station

Carfax Tower where the Mountaineering club managed to souvenir the Red Flag.

one dark winters evening and greeted the arrival of a train with enthusiastic cries of "All Change for Liverpool!". In wartime people were used to such inconveniences and soon the passengers were swarming onto the platform. It so happened that this was in fact the Liverpool train so confusion reigned supreme as furious travellers floundered about trying to regain their seats. Unfortunately we were told that Simon had taken a swing at the policeman who tried to stop him and spent the night in the cooler.

Towards the end of the year, with November 5th approaching, the Balliol men hung a realistic Guy, dressed in an Auxiliary Fireman's uniform, from a gibbet over the College gateway in the Broad which gave some early morning passers by a bit of a turn. It took the College staff some time to get it down but it reappeared the next morning hanging opposite the Randolph Hotel with what the local paper coyly called "a household utensil" embellishing it. For a nasty moment we thought that perhaps the good Hodgens had found the frustrations of running the Balliol Fire Unit from Trinity too much for him.

CHAPTER NINE

The first term at Trinity, Michaelmas 1940, had seemed a bit of a muddle. So many things had to be learnt, so many new faces, so much readjustment after the several months of non-academic freedom. I had left school in May 1939 because after I had passed School Certificate with the requisite number of credits to enter University, my father thought it would do me more good to see a bit of the world than sit around for another year in the sixth form. So I had joined my parents in Kashmir, where my father was then Director of Medical Services, and because of the outbreak of war, had not been able to get back home until March 1940. Then there had been the fall of France, enrolment in the LDV which became the Home Guard, swatting at the crammer for the Balliol entrance exam, then the Blitz and all its attendant excitements. But by the end of the Hilary term things had settled down, a circle of friends established, and a place in the scheme of things. On staircase eleven we had a close little circle of Paddy Engelbach, David Marsh, Vernon St John and me. We used to crouch round the fire in either my or Paddy's room pooling our meagre ration of coal. Others frequently joined us –David Humphreys, Nigel Mathew, David Aiers, Ray Peters– and other more casual acquaintances from the other staircases. Here, when we weren't otherwise engaged in outside activities, we would gossip the evenings away, puffing at our cigarettes or newly acquired pipes. Smoking was central to our way of life. The first move of social contact was always to offer the new-comer a cigarette. Most of us kept a cigarette box on the table for this purpose and we all proudly possessed cigarette cases and lighters of various distinction.

My father had given me a silver cigarette case for my seventeenth birthday. It could hold ten Turkish or Egyptian cigarettes but not the fat round Virginian. I had become used to the run-of-the-mill packet cigarettes in the Home Guard where one of our members called Middleditch was the advertising manager for Kensitas and therefore kept us supplied with the packets of twenty that had a picture of a butler on them and an extra piece stuck on containing "four for your friends." On the way out to India we used to stock up with Markovitch Black & White Virginian in round tins of fifty which we bought in Aden for 1/6 a tin. At home we used to keep a supply of fat round hand-made cigarettes bought from the Army and Navy Stores. But for choice we preferred the flat Turkish brands or their like. As they became scarcer, Nevil and I favoured a brand of Cyprus cigarettes labelled Kuprinos, which came in rather pretty little cardboard boxes. They also fitted my silver cigarette case which I used to proffer with a practised hand, pressing the clip so that it flew open with the contents facing the person being offered. It was only later that the crumpled packet of Players became a regular accompaniment of our lives.

I think it was Paddy who started the move into pipes. Possibly it was because his boxing trainers had persuaded him that cigarettes were bad for fitness or it might have been that he fancied himself with a pipe in his mouth looking manly and responsible, a ploy used by Stanley Baldwin and later Harold Wilson. Anyway pipes suddenly became the thing. Paddy, after some experiment, chose a sort of meerschaum which hung easily out of the side of his mouth. I ended up with a straight stemmed affair that required me to clench my teeth in the approved Bulldog Drummond manner with what I imagined was a manly expression. I soon discovered that pipe smoking was not only time consuming but expensive. The paraphernalia required included a tobacco pouch and an endless supply of matches - Swan Vestas with the sand paper down only one side were the approved model. Then there was the drawn out ritual of filling the bowl with tobacco, tamping it in and setting it alight. The popular tobacco of the day was called "Baby's Bottom", advertised as "being as smooth as". I found that either the pipe refused to light because I had packed it too tightly, or lit like a fuse and sent shafts of fire along the stem which burnt my tongue. I hated it. After a few weeks of battling with alternate fire and frustration I relegated my pipe to a prominent position on my mantelpiece where it proclaimed my manly intentions without further testing my patience.

Apart from the joys of smoking, we regularly went to a barber's shop down the Turl where you could get a haircut, shampoo and shave for 4/6, complete with hot towels and the application of an astringent that made you think your head had shrunk. It was visits to this establishment that solved one of the war's most irritating problems, the shortage of razor blades. Blue Gillette, the most popular blade of the day, vanished from the shelves fairly early on to be superceded by things called Seven O'Clock and ultimately nameless pieces of metal that went blunt as soon as you unwrapped them from their greasy bits of paper.

There were many ingenious methods of trying to keep razor blades sharp. My father had acquired a whole range of gadgets from a sort of box in which he used to click the blade up and down to a marvellous little thing in which you could enclose the blade and pull it up and down a piece of string which rotated a series of tiny whetstones. Paddy had read that a blade could be kept sharp by rubbing it on the inside of a glass tumbler and there was yet another gadget which worked up and down an ordinary razor strop. But if one was going to have an ordinary razor strop surely the logical thing would be to have an ordinary razor, like a cut-throat. So I watched carefully how the barber went about it and asked him to show me how. Then I bought one to try it out. After the vain scrapings with blunt safety blades it worked beautifully. I soon found that it was possible to avoid all sorts of blips much more effectively than with a so-called "safety". Eventually I equipped myself with two razors so that I could put one in for resetting. Correctly, I was told, you should have eight razors, one for each day of the week and one being reset, but my two trusty blades lasted me through the rest of the war and long after. I was surprised that no-one else seemed inclined to copy me but they may have been put off by Paddy's solitary effort. He borrowed my razor after a brief period of instruction but managed to inflict upon himself enough cuts and slashes as to daunt the most determined copyist. Strangely, in spite of people like Derek Bibby being in the University Naval Squadron, it never seemed to occur to us to grow beards but probably, now that we were technically soldiers, the STC would have forbidden it.

Perhaps the most remarkable thing about life in college during this time was that it was so unremarkable. A short piece that appeared in the Cherwell of 2nd May 41 gives a light-hearted but not inaccurate contemporary account of undergraduate life. It was called "The Day's Work".

> "Twelve minutes to eight, sir; quite a nice morning!" Just before I fell asleep again I heard his voice in the next room, more distant. "Twelve minutes to eight, sir; quite a nice morning!" And so it went on, fainter and fainter, like a series of ballroom mirrors in a Metro-Goldwyn-Mayer film. (Rather a good simile, don't you think?)
> I had meant to get up early this morning and have a bath before breakfast for once. I set my alarm-clock for seven-thirty but never heard it go off. (By the way, it's a fine little clock; luminous, eight days, Swiss, and very expensive. It isn't mine; it belongs to a chap who's gone in the army.) I woke again at ten past eight, sprang out of bed, had a hurried bath and was just finishing the trousers when I woke and found I was still in bed. Added to which it was ten to nine. Missed breakfast again, of course. Nine-thirty my scout came in. "Cor Christ Church! You still in bed!" I must have been because he came in again at half past ten and I certainly wasn't up. I sat on the edge of the bed, drawing on an idle sock and muttering about the possibilities of getting a bath.
> "Shouldn't worry about a bath at this time of the morning." It was quite unnecessary, quite uncalled for, but then Frank is like that.
> I breakfasted in my dressing gown off Heinz Sandwich Spread (very difficult to get these days; I got the last jar

from the JCR), bread, and apricot jam. I also made a cup of china tea in my magic spoon. (It's a sort of infusor, instead of a tea-pot. I don't really like china tea, but one or two people who drop in for tea like it so I usually get it.) I switched on my wireless set while I was dressing and listened to Christopher Stone talking about to-day's anniversaries. He played "Si mes vers avaient des ailes" because it was Victor Hugo's birthday. I suppose he must have written the words or something. Incidentally it's a very nice wireless set (I hate calling them radios), polished walnut I believe. It isn't mine, it belongs to a chap who's gone in the army.

I went into the library when I was dressed, chiefly because there is a fire there and I want to save my coal. I sort of fell asleep until lunch-time, but I was aware all the time of a man sitting opposite me who annoyed me intensely. He kept slamming books about and poking the fire. I expect he guessed I had a pretty late night and was trying to wake me up but I wasn't having any.

I had lunch in Hall. Two evil little fish on toast, with nasty squiggly bones in them. I went back to the library afterwards and read one or two things. Then I went out to buy a gramophone record. It was tea-time before I had chosen one (I generally hear a few when I go in) so I dashed up to Somerville to have tea with Helen. (That's not her real name, but she's so funny, I have to be very careful these days.) We had boiled eggs and she played a record of Hutch singing "All the things you are" on her gramophone. (I say her gramophone, but actually it belongs to a man in Magdalen.) I refused a cigarette because I had a cold, and she called me a sissy. I said I supposed she wanted some frightfully strong man with hairs all over the place, and she said I was rude. I said she was a prude. Anyway she's not my girl, she belongs to a fellow who's gone in the army.

I left at six fifty-five and fairly raced down the Corn because the steward looks so snooty if you roll in late for dinner.

I went to the Randolph after dinner to meet Sheila as arranged. (That really is her name, but I know she won't mind.) We swilled some coffee together and as she was paying for it I let her have all the sugar while I used saccharin. I took her back to St Hilda's and then raced down to the Mitre and swilled some more coffee with Helen. (We arranged this this afternoon.) She'd brought a book along with a lot of funny pictures in and we roared with laughter all the time. My cold seemed to be getting worse so I didn't take her back to Somerville. Instead I gave her my torch and she lent me her gloves because I had left one of mine in a certain place a few days ago. I told her this and she laughed.

I went back to College and went straight to bed with a hot water bottle. I also took two aspros (not aspirins) and lay awake till three wondering whether they'd affect my heart."

Not many of us were quite as caddish as Casus, the anonymous author, but it catches the contemporary atmosphere quite well.

Friendships were occasionally strained as when Paddy left a party early. He had had far too much to drink and I was worried that he might not have made it back to his room. When I looked in on him he was lying on his back on his bed smiling seraphically.

"I've been sick," he announced smugly. I looked round his room.

"No you haven't," I said, "You've imagined it."

"In your room," he said with a delighted grin.

I rushed back to my room and indeed Paddy was right, he had been comprehensively sick in my basin, my po, and on my bedside rug.

I went back to his room.

"You can bloody well come and clean it up," I demanded.

"North'll do it. Good old North." Whereupon he passed out and either couldn't be or was determined not to be wakened. I retrieved much of the damage by swopping basins and pos with the sleeping Paddy and rolled up the bedside carpet. The strains of communal living. It wasn't as bad as the umbrage in St John's when Philip Larkin accused his room mate of shitting in his shoe.

But there was a great deal of camerarderie. We looked after each other. Drunks were carried back to their rooms and put to bed. Hangovers were treated with tenderness and respect and genuine illness attracted a commendable level of concerned attention and recommended remedies from simple aspirin to elaborately concocted hot toddies. When Nevil Macready decided that the pavement of St John Street was an excellent place to lie down and sleep, he was borne back to his rooms in such exemplary manner that it was difficult to persuade him later that he had ever wished to lie anywhere else, and Paddy, having decided to experiment with the effects of port, was found peacefully asleep on a bench in Beaumont Street with the port bottle still clutched to his bosom. He too was delivered to his room without mishap. Nevil was treated with great tenderness by the assembled gathering when he misjudged the speed of a blacked out lorry in the Giler and was bounced unceremoniously onto the street. It was generally agreed though that if he had been sober he might have been quite badly hurt.

There were, of course, quieter evenings when we immersed ourselves in our books, wrote our essays or spent the evening after dinner in Hall in one or other's room listening to music, talking about what we might do after the war, and occasionally reading our poems to each other. We all wrote poetry of a kind. The spirit of Rupert Brooke was still very much alive in our generation, the thought that "If I should die —." Paddy's friend Sidney Keyes was generally being hailed as the "modern Rupert Brooke" but it is difficult to claim that his poetry was truly the voice of his generation. Sadly he emulated his predecessor by being killed in North Africa whilst serving as a Platoon Commander with the Queen's Own Royal West Kent Regiment.

Listening to classical music on twelve inch 78s being played on a wind-up HMV portable is not as relaxing as it ought to be because every four minutes you had to change the record, wind up the machine, and, if you were properly conscientious, change the needle. Never-the-less we managed to enjoy the works in a manner which enabled us to repeat favourite passages as soon as we heard them. Paddy's favourite was "Til Eulenspiegel" because there was a passage near the end which was supposed to represent someone being beheaded. "Listen to this, listen to this!" he would cry and play the passage again, miming the action with a chopping motion of his hand and pausing for the bomp-bomp of the tympany that was supposed to depict the victim's head bouncing onto the scaffold. Then Paddy would roar with laughter, dance around, and put the passage on again.

In our more introspective moments we would listen to "The Swan of Tuonela" or, one of our favourites, the wonderful recording of Elgar conducting his own Violin Concerto with the young Yehudi Menuhin as soloist. The recently released Walt Disney film, "Fantasia" had popularised "Night on Bare Mountain" which we used to call music to puff smoke rings to. Then to cheer ourselves up I would go and fetch Artie Shaw's "One Night Stand" or "Carioca" and David would inevitably get his pile of Deanna Durbins.

Reggie Barr's production of "Othello" was scheduled to open on March 5th. Having started as a Trinity and Christ Church venture it now became a production for the Friends of the OUDS but, because the Friends of the OUDS was not registered as an official organisation, it was necessary to find a sponsoring organisation to enable the Taylorian to be obtained. The Conservative Association came to the rescue thus circumventing the extraordinary sets of rules and regulations that seemed designed as much to thwart as to assist any student endeavours.

The stage in the Taylorian Institute had been designed for lectures and demonstrations. It was about fourteen feet deep and twenty-two feet across. On each side a door led on to a flight of stairs which went down to a basement area where two dressing rooms opened off a cramped communal area which was directly under the stage. It would have been fine for a solo pianist to have a wash and brush up between sonatas but as a facility for a full scale Shakespearean production it left much to be desired. Perhaps if the modern method of open staging had been used, it might have been easier, but in those days you had to have curtains and these were strung across the front of the stage with a border to create a semblance of a proscenium. The audience had to sit on upright wooden chairs without the benefit of tiers, so that even with careful alternating of the rows to try to provide gaps, the back rows had difficulty seeing. There was a balcony that did have some tiered seating but very few rows. So those that felt that University theatre ought to be encouraged bravely endured cramp and numbed posteriors to do so.

Because of other commitments, it was only possible to get into the Hall the day before the opening for a dress rehearsal. Curtains and flats were housed in the old Playhouse building in the Woodstock Road and had to be trundled to the Taylorian in a hand cart borrowed from the Trinity lodge. So the dress rehearsal took place in an atmosphere of improvisation as the stage crew valiantly tried to rig the set and lights. As has been said in another context, it was not so much that the thing was done well as that it was done at all.

In spite of having boasted that it would be an all undergraduate production breaking with the past, Reggie had employed a young professional actress to play Desdemona. He dismissed my suggestion that surely he could have found someone from one of the women's colleges by simply saying, "Have you seen them?" He also enlisted another professional, Rosamund Kennedy, to play Emilia. Costumes for the show came from the stocks of Fox or Berman and to a remarkable extent seemed to fit. While we struggled into our various disguises, Geoffrey Bennison was still fitting up his set which consisted of a rostrum across the back from which steps led down onto the main acting area through a series of arches. Wing flats could be brailed back to provide an enclosed set.

I had prepared myself for my small part with all the enthusiasm of the novice amateur. From the Leichner shop, next door to the Empire Theatre in Leicester Square, I had equipped myself with sticks of 5 and 9, two shades of carmine, lake, blue and brown liners, a can of cocoanut butter, a box of blending powder and a hare's foot. I put the make-up in a cigar box of my father's and arrived at the hall with the lot neatly wrapped up in a small face towel. Any idea I may have had that I would be able

The Taylorian Stage.

The Taylorian Auditorium, The same old upright wooden chairs.

Roderigo (Mr. John Eyre), Emelia (Miss. Rosamund Kennedy), and Iago (Mr. Derek Brinson) in a scene from "Othello", given in the Taylorian, Oxford, by the Friends of the O.U.D.S.

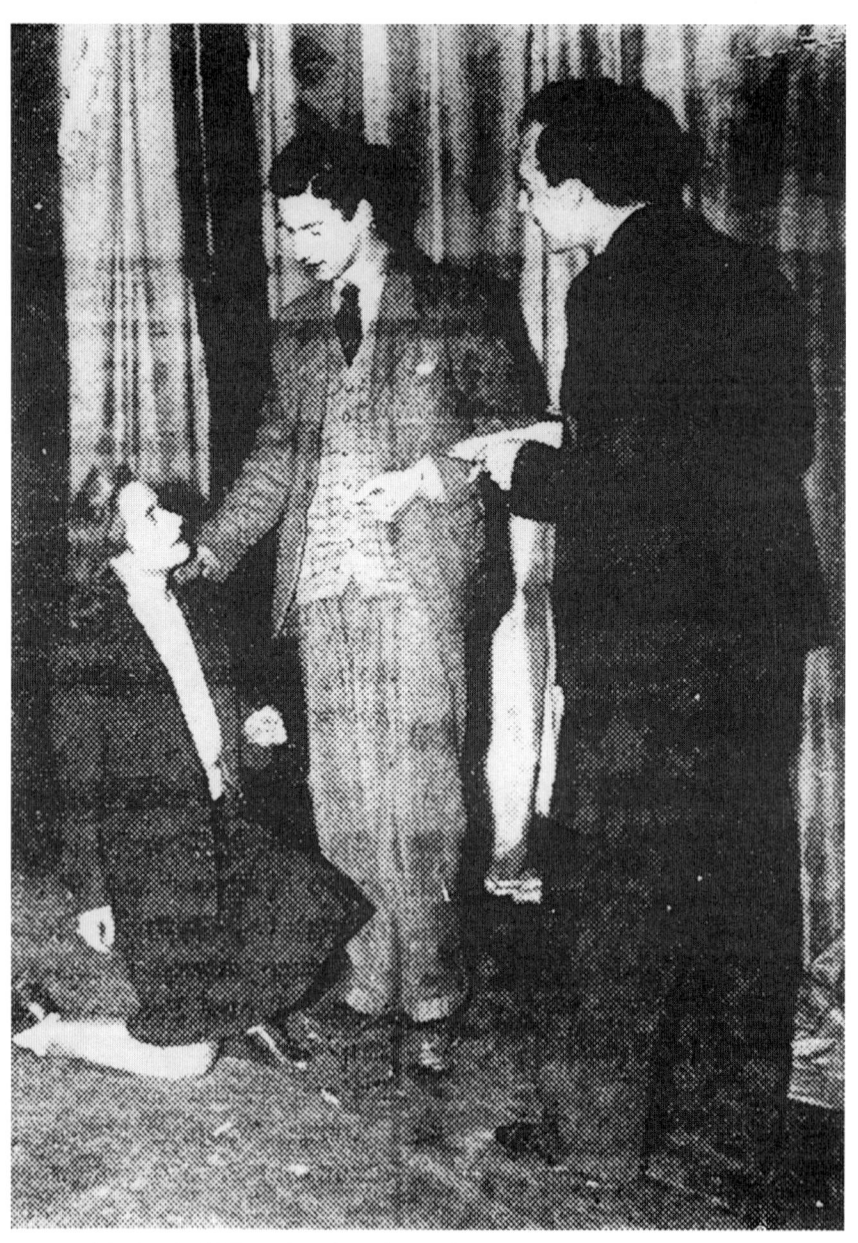

Mr Reginald Barr (producer) watching Miss Jeanette Tregarthen ("Desdemona") and Mr Derek Brinson ("Iago") during a rehearsal by the O.U.D.S. of "Othello".

to lay my gear out on a dressing table in front of a lighted dressing-room mirror was soon dispelled when it became clear that all the dressing room space would be required for the leading players and the rest of us would have to do with pocket mirrors propped up on chairs. I had practised putting on my make-up in my room at Trinity with a book on "The Art of Make-up" encouraging me to recreate my fairly undistinguished features. After the dress rehearsal, at the risk of being followed, I made up and changed in college and strode boldly round to the Taylorian clutching my box of blending powder to take the shine off my exertions. As the show progressed I must have been the most over-dressed stage hand in history.

To give him his due, Reggie's Othello wasn't a bad stab at it in spite of the tendency of his black fuzzy wig to slip back and reveal a tell-tale white line across his furrowed brow. He spoke the lines beautifully and had a good commanding presence. Derek Brinson was a subtly smarmy Iago and Derek Morphett a nicely romantic Cassio. John Eyre played John Gielgud playing Roderigo and Michael Flanders quietly stole his part of the show as Brabantio. Jeanette Tregarthen as Desdemona was far too cool and passionless until, after the first night, Reggie became enraged at her lack of fire and gave her a resounding slap on the face which brought tears to her eyes and a satisfactory rise in the tempo of her performance.

The subsequent reviews were nothing if not critical. Michael Meyer enjoyed himself in the Cherwell. "Othello, in his first appearance, wore a fearful turban which made him look like the Commissionaire at the Taj Mahal. Mr Michael Flanders (Brabantio) was the best of the other characters." Peter Bayley was "an inadequate Duke." The Oxford Magazine wrote "Mr Barr, who strongly resembled the unfortunate African Emperor now happily on the way back to his throne" also castigated Desdemona for acting "within the famous gamut of A to B". My own short burst when I dashed eagerly down the steps in a hat that made me look like a cocker spaniel received some notice, Michael Meyer writing "The messenger at Cyprus, who bears the glad tidings of peace to a weary people, might have been the grocer's boy bringing the good news to Newton Abbot for all the impression he made on his listeners." I hoped he was referring to the lack of reaction of the cast, not my unrestrained piece of over-acting. Nevertheless it was a brave try and greeted by the Oxford Mail as " a bold feat to tackle Othello in wartime on the limited stage of the Taylor Institute." We did four performances, opening on Wednesday, 5th March at 7.30 p.m., a matinee on Thursday at 2.30 and evening performances on Friday and Saturday. I seem to remember that the stage had to be cleared after the Thursday afternoon show for some other function that had been previously booked. Tickets were 2/6 and 1/6!

In all the excitement of preparing for Othello I had not noticed that Paddy Engelbach had disappeared. The next time I saw him was at breakfast on Friday morning looking as if he had been run over by a bus. He had been over to Cambridge with the University boxing team for the annual contest that took place the day after our first night. Cambridge had won and our three Trinity contenders lost their fights. Peter Balmer lost to I.J. Abrahams and Nigel Mathew to S.A. Garibian on points but poor Paddy had his fight with V.C. Waterstone stopped in the third round. He may have lost his fight but he had won his Blue which was all that mattered.

As the term came to a close we were all engaged in the various exams which constituted a Wartime Degree. Having wasted my first term I was lucky that my first exam on Shakespeare and his period was a fairly easily surmounted hurdle with the liberal aid of Granville Barker, Reggie's discarded essays, memories of Margaret Rawlings, brought together by the gentle coaxing of Nevill Coghill. Meanwhile plans were being made for the coming vacation.

Nevill, Paddy and I were going up to Morecambe to collect the girls and take them to Mull which involved getting special passes organised, green identity cards, temporary ration cards and all the paraphernalia of wartime travel. Reggie didn't seem to have any special plans but in the last week became very secretive as he was expecting a visit from a girl friend. She came to his rooms and all of us were given clear orders to keep away. We were allowed the briefest of introductions and sportingly made our excuses. She was very slim with short fair hair and seemed tall for a ballet dancer. I don't think that he had a great deal of success as he complained afterwards that dancers were difficult to seduce because they had such strong thigh muscles. It was the only time I met Beryl Grey. However Reggie obviously had other strings to his bow as, on the 28th March, the Dean recorded that he cautioned Barr, Rampton, R.A. Taylor and MacPherson for being seen leaving college at ten p.m. with two lady visitors.

As a postscript to Hilary 41, the Conservative Association took over the Cherwell magazine and we saw the last of Stanley Parker's attractive covers. It was a form of curtain falling at the end of the play.

CHAPTER TEN

As soon as the term ended I joined Margaret in London and Nevil joined his parents in the considerable comfort of the Park Lane Hotel. This was a billet compatible with his father's exalted position as Vice Chief of the Imperial General Staff or, more prosaically, second head of the Army. Nevil's mother was French, a relative of the Comte de Noailles, whose well-known poem on Verdun I had once had to translate for an exam. She was involved in organising support for the Free French Forces based in Britain under the command of General de Gaulle. One such function was a reception and cabaret for which she asked me to produce a small band to play for dancing. I immediately sought out Len Hunt in Archer Street.

This short and undistinguished street runs parallel to Shaftesbury Avenue between Great Windmill Street and Berwick Street. Apart from the stage doors of three theatres, including the famous Windmill, it houses the headquarters of the Musician's Union and the Musician's Club. During the great Dance Band era the street would be crowded with musicians, some of them hopefully wearing their dinner jackets and black ties, looking for gig work or even full time employment. Even in wartime there was a considerable turn out of young and not so young hopefuls.

Opposite the Musician's Club and sandwiched between the backs of the Lyric and Queen's Theatres, there was a sleazy tenement building. In the basement there was an out-of-hours drinking club. Above that were three floors of mysterious doors with multiple padlocks, and on the top floor Len had leased a room in which he had installed a lathe on which he made drum sticks and another machine for making wire brushes. His partner at the time was Bud Carter-Mather who was one of the two resident drummers at the Windmill, working alternate shows which gave him two hour breaks to help with the manufacturing. From such humble beginnings began the subsequently prosperous L.W. Hunt Drum Manufacturing Company. Len had no trouble fixing things and the Harper-Nelson Trio consisted of the legendary E.O. "Eddie" Pogson on clarinet and saxophone, and Alec Blackford on piano and me on the drums. We played for three hours for the handsome fee of nine guineas. It was my first paid job. During the cabaret we had a break when we were served sandwiches and wine. Poggy, who had toured Europe with the Jack Hylton Band before the war, sniffed the proffered claret with the air of an expert, pronounced it to be red ink and asked for beer. He then regaled us with stories of his adventures on tour which made the world of show business seem to be the most glamourous and exciting way of life.

Nevil too was bitten by the bug, although his family were not too keen in spite of his being the great great grandson of the Great Macready. Perhaps that was why. His friend Esmund Seal had worked in films as an editor and intended to make it his career and Nevil and I had gone to the cinema as often as possible, occasionally submitting our critiques to the Cherwell for publication. It was a period of considerable quality in film making typified to-day by the revival of films like "Casablanca".

There were the brilliant Preston Sturges comedies with a social sting like "The Lady Eve" and "Sullivan's Travels", the light sophisticated Thin Man series with Myrna Loy and William Powell, Chaplin had weighed in with "The Great Dictator" and there were the heavier dramas such as the "Grapes of Wrath" and "Of Mice and Men", while down Walton Street we went to the Scala to wallow in films made by Renoir, Cocteau and Marcel Carne. Infuriatingly Nevil spoke fluent French and didn't need to read the subtitles so that he kept laughing at jokes I hadn't understood. They must have been oldish films because France had been over-run by the Germans since early 1940 but "La Bete Humaine", "Le Million", and others persuaded us that the French had an intellectual component which American, and certainly British, films lacked. Most of us went to the pictures twice a week as a matter of course and naturally considered ourselves experts so that analytical discussions on the merits of this or that director, cameraman, writer, designer or actor sometimes went on late into the night. If there was one dominating theme in Oxford in 1941 it was the desire to talk.

Sometimes our choice of film was influenced by our musical interests. Artie Shaw's band was featured in "Second Chorus", Glen Miller's in "Sun Valley Serenade", Jimmy Lunceford in "Blues in the Night", Fats Waller in "Syncopation" and Bob Crosby in "Cis Hopkins." In this last film I spotted a girl playing a supporting role to whom I wrote a fan letter after some challenging from Nevil and Paddy. As a result I received a snapshot of my pin-up posed in a bathing costume by a swimming pool signed "For John, Good Luck, Susan Hayward". It became my mascot and I have carried it with me ever since.

Stage struck and film struck it was inevitable that we should decide to see for ourselves. Fortunately the son of the former cricket professional at Cheltenham College was running

Battered by over 50 years in my wallet -my mascot.

Central Casting in London so any Old Cheltonian could get a job as a film extra if his curiosity got the better of him. So Nevil and I duly queued up on the stairs of a shabby office off Leicester Square to be allotted two days work as film extras. The next morning found us huddled coldly on the platform at Marylebone Station to catch the 7.15 train for Denham. We had been told to wear light suits as we were going to be in Italy. We had been warned not to take anything valuable with us to the studios as film extras were recruited from a pretty unreliable sector of society so we shunned the huge extras' changing room and reported to the assistant director who ushered us on to the set. The film was called "The First of the Few" and we had to sit at tables in a cafe overlooking a canal in Venice. The set was totally realistic even to having a gondola in a water filled canal to be paddled up to a landing stage. The director was Anthony Asquith and the stars we watched performing were Leslie Howard and David Niven. We were fascinated by the whole thing, especially the fact that nothing much seemed to be happening. So we learnt straight away that film making is mostly hanging around while mysterious technical problems are solved. While various mutterings went on round the camera, Asquith, Howard and Niven went up onto the full size replica of the Bridge of Sighs (the Venetian not the Oxford one) and held a yodelling contest. In due course we were called to silence, everyone took their allotted places and the gondola scene was shot and shot again and then again from every conceivable angle. At no time did the camera seem to face in our direction so we soon gave up pretending to be Italians and simply watched the proceedings. It took all day to film the short scene and then we queued up to be paid two guineas each. It seemed a pretty easy way to make a living. As we left we were asked if we had dinner jackets and were told to wear them. So once more we caught the 7.15, nodding to one or two of our colleagues of the previous day. It made us feel like old hands.

This time we were in a much larger crowd. It was a huge reception being held in Canberra, Australia, to welcome the flyer Amy Johnson after her record breaking flight from Britain. Herbert Wilcox was the director and somewhere in the melee we were told that Anna Neagle was making a speech. The film was called "She Flew Alone" and once again neither of us seemed destined for stardom although a camera on a crane did pass over our heads. For wearing our own dinner jackets we qualified for four guineas for the day. That concluded our careers as film extras.

Nevil, Paddy and I had caught up with the Hulbert Follies in Morecambe where they were playing in the Winter Garden Theatre for a week before taking an Easter break. The town was swarming with RAF recruits being shouted through their basic training but we must have found billets for ourselves somewhere. The Winter Garden was a huge place and one of the few theatres where even Cicely Courtneidge was glad to be provided with a microphone. But microphones were less reliable then so that, during the show we saw, someone in the back of the audience shouted, "We can't hear you!". "Can't hear me?. shouted Cis, "Thanks for letting me know." Whereupon the old trouper turned on the full volume and no one had any trouble hearing her or the rest of the cast.

Back stage after the performance we met Laurence Green again and the stage manager George Pughe who told us about the difficulty they were having with back stage crew. In Morecambe they had a crew of eager RAF recruits, but in many towns there were few regulars and the part timers were often unavailable at short notice if the Air Raid siren went or the shops they served in were open. They asked us if we would like to join them. Obviously we wouldn't be able to do so until the long vacation but Nevil and I jumped at the opportunity. Paddy had organised some flying training and had to decline. I suspect that the thought of having a descendant of the Great Macready as an Assistant Stage Manager may have influenced their offer.

Only Cynthia managed to get to Mull. The four of us did all the usual sight- seeing trips to Iona and Tobermory happily using our generous supply of petrol. Then Cynthia had to head off South to rejoin the show and we spent the next week lazing about and listening endlessly to the wireless.

From five until six every evening, the BBC broadcast dance music. This was mostly provided by their resident dance band

Cynthia with Nevil Macready outside the Abbey in Iona.

Me, Annabel, Paddy & Nevil

Nevil, me & Paddy with Romeo

directed by Henry Hall but from time to time other leading bands of the day were featured; Harry Roy, Joe Loss, Ambrose, Eric Winstone, Geraldo, Lew Stone, Maurice Winnick, Billy Cotton. Then once a week they acknowledged the popularity of the Rhythm Clubs by presenting Harry Parry and The Radio Rhythm Club Sextet which included the young George Shearing. There was strict tempo dance music complete with lessons provided by Victor Sylvester and occasionally Josephine Bradley. Because of copyright and Union restrictions we never heard American bands although their arrangements were freely used by the British bands. For example, "In The Mood" was a national hit for Joe Loss before most people had even heard of Glen Miller. And each evening in the comfortable warmth of the oil lamps with the black-out curtains carefully drawn, we used to listen to the regular supply of comedy shows. Jack Warner starred in "Garrison Theatre" making "Mind my bike" a national catch phrase, Tommy Handley had just started his long running series of "It's That Man Again", Flanagan and Allen had a short series which introduced us to Nettlerash, a sort of Cockney McGonnigal, whose tortured verses and absurdly strained rhymes had Nevil so doubled up with laughter that he fell off his chair. Saturday Nights had Music Hall where you could hear some of the stars who spent their lives touring the provinces as top of the bill in variety shows. Nosmo King, Oliver Wakefield, Gillie Potter, Cavan O'Connor, Florence Desmond, Clapham and Dwyer, Ronald Frankau, Anne Ziegler and Webster Booth, Max Miller, Leslie Hutchinson "Hutch", Turner Layton and Vic Oliver all took their turn in our beehive Murphy radio with that mysterious green eye that was supposed to indicate that you were perfectly tuned. The set was powered by a big heavy dry battery and an accumulator which had to be kept topped up with distilled water and recharged from the electric lighting plant. Ironically we had to use the oils lamps at night if we wanted to listen to the wireless because the noise of the electricity plant was picked up and drowned the reception.

In Mull, on rare occasions we could faintly hear an American station called Schenechtady but for news of America we relied on the muffled tones and static ridden voice of Raymond Gram Swing. In between all this we had the news read for us in measured tones by the impeccable public school accents of Stuart Hibbert, Joseph MacLeod, Alvar Liddell, and Bruce Belfrage who barely paused in his bulletin when Broadcasting House received a direct hit while he was reading the news. By necessity our radio was entirely British but our film-going and much of our chosen reading was heavily American.

When the production of "Heil Hitler" fell through, Reggie Barr recruited us to do a reading of Maxwell Anderson's "Winterset". Gordon Davies, Derek Morphett, Reggie and I sat in front of the fire doing our best American accents as learnt off the movies. "You lousy roost of punks and gulls" became one of our favourite terms of abuse. But we were all more or less Yankiphiles as far as literature was concerned. Hemingway, Steinbeck, O'Hara, O'Neill, O'Casey and even the saccharin Saroyan were much read and admired either as novelists or playwrights. But the writers who most influenced our style of humour and even modes of speech were H. Allen Smith, S.J. Perelman, James Thurber, and Damon Runyon. "Life in a Putty Knife Factory", "Crazy Like A Fox", "The Thurber Carnival" were constantly quoted and, of course, I had won the short story competition with a Runyon parody. "I am in Elliston's when who should come in but —", Nevil Macready would say as he recounted some casual meeting. There were some strange cadences to be heard as we spouted Runyonesque constructions in our fashionable Oxford drawls. This admiration for things American was reinforced by the presence of a group of Americans who chose not to flee to the safety of neutrality and remained in London to broadcast and perform. Bebe Daniels and Ben Lyon, with Vic Oliver, who sensibly married Churchill's daughter, combined to produce the morale raising show "Hi Gang" bringing to the BBC the exuberance of American broadcasting which we later experienced when we began to hear the Bob Hope and Jack Benny Shows. They never outclassed the mad illogicality of I.T.M.A. though, which somehow reflected the uniquely British attitudes to the war and its idiotic inconveniences. So we still clung to our own standards of humour through radio, while appreciating the American influence, and isolated in Mull our reliance on radio became much more accentuated. But where-ever we were it is true to say that the entire nation ground to a halt each evening for the six o'clock news.

Our cosy sojourn soon came to an end and we sailed back to Oban on the little Lochinvar with its friendly smell of diesel oil and boiled potatoes, through the lines of merchant shipping, past the Sunderlands and Catalinas swinging at their anchors in Oban Bay, to catch the midday train that would puff and splutter its way up the hill to Connell Ferry, past Loch Awe and high over Rannoch Moor to Stirling, Carlisle and the South. The Summer of our Trinity term lay ahead.

CHAPTER ELEVEN

The first obvious difference in life at the beginning of the Trinity Term was that we could see. The days had lengthened and the petty irritations of the black-out no longer entirely governed our lives. The less petty irritation of the STC remained and we were soon to be seen in scattered squads advancing across Christ Church meadows, hurling ourselves down at yells of "Under Fire!" crawling past the cowpats which were becoming depressingly familiar - down, crawl, observe, fire - if the Gemans had landed could the OUSTC have held the line of the Cherwell? Then we queued to return our rifles to the armoury before clattering back to our colleges. It was hard to equate these frenetic activities with the tranquillity that the Reverend Dodgson must have found as he strolled along the Broad Walk to the banks of the Isis. But with the coming of Summer the river had sprung to life. Punts crowded the waterways, college eights bore down on them with shrill cries of "Look Ahead!", canoes careered cheerfully through the throng. The scene below Magdalen Bridge on May morning was almost mediaeval in its colourful confusion. Paddy and I had acquired a punt for the traditional greeting at dawn on the 1st May by the choir of Magdalen College singing from the College tower. Without amplification it was faintly possible to detect a thin tinkling sound but whatever sound there was was covered by the bumping of the boats against eachother and the murmur of the assembled crowd.

After our more or less monastic existence of the previous terms we had also found girls to join us. Pamela MacKenzie had been a neighbour in Dolphin Square where she lived with

May morning at Oxford: The Cherwell was crowded with punts at 6 a.m. this morning, when the choirboys sang from Magdalen College Tower.
Oxford Mail 1 May 1941.

her widowed mother and had shared the air raid shelter. Now she was working with MI5 whose offices had mysteriously moved into Keble College. There was something of an irony about this as Keble College was regarded as an Anglican seminary where would-be parsons studied Theology in a five year course. It was generally seen as a clever way to avoid being called up without having to pretend to be a conscientious objector because, for some odd reason, parsons were treated like doctors and were exempt during the course of their training. The effect of these religious draft dodgers on the Church of England would only become apparent some thirty years later. Medical students were the only others who were allowed to complete their full course of training before being liable to be called up, but it was never suggested that anyone became a Doctor in the hope of avoiding the war.

Paddy's friend was Ursula Cartledge. I can't remember whether she was with the Slade School of Art or Westfield, but I think that Paddy had found her when he was changing gramophone records in the library. It was probably the Slade because the following March she was congratulated, with a Mr Willner, for 'the charming scenery" for H.M.S. Pinafore but I know that music was a mutual interest. Anyway it added a decorative dimension to our messing about in boats. For the next few weeks the river played a considerable part in our lives. Three or four of us would hire a punt at Folly Bridge and go off with a gramophone and picnic to wend our way up the Cherwell. If there were girls in the party they had to get out and walk while the men took the punt past the section of the river known as Parson's Pleasure. This was a nude bathing area for men only. On the whole the men on display were a pretty unlovely lot so that it's probably just as well they were concealed from the girls who might have been considerably disillusioned. There was a slipway where the punts could be hauled over rollers to the upper reaches of the river where it ran past the University Parks, thus avoiding the vision of naked dons.

 I have to confess that few of us actually punted using the pole provided. Punting is an art which has to be learnt if you don't want to go round endlessly in circles. Even if you have mastered the art of going straight, there is the constant hazard of falling overboard. This can be achieved by simply losing one's balance when the boat gives a sudden lurch, or by the pole sticking in the mud so that the punt glides on while the punter is left hanging helplessly onto the pole. Once this happens there is an awful inevitability about the ensuing pantomime. For a short time the punter clings to the pole while his passengers try to paddle back to him, but getting a moving punt into reverse is a slow business, not made easier by the merry laughter of the onlookers as punter and pole subside slowly into the river.

 There was another hazard on the Cherwell which was a strand of cable which stretched across the river from Christ Church meadows to the opposite bank to guide a small hand-propelled ferry. It is incredibly difficult to judge the distance of a horizontal wire as Paddy found when he was showing off his punting prowess to an admiring Ursula. One minute he was standing confidently in the stern propelling his charge to the prospective confines of some selected shady bank, when suddenly, with a satisfactory twang, he was catapulted into the murky depths. Most of us therefore contented ourselves by using the paddles provided.

Sometimes we would go upstream through a lock above Folly Bridge along a fairly unsalubrious section of canal until the river widened and we reached a landing stage that fronted the lawns of a pub called the Perch. It was all very Edwardian, Jerome K. Jerome, even to our dress of grey flannels, cricket shirts and college blazers. The summer of 1941, like its predecessor, was halcyon, but as we enjoyed these peaceful pursuits the centre of London was visited by one of its worst raids on the night of May 10th, and elsewhere the war rumbled on. We watched the fires reflected on the clouds forty miles away and then turned again to the river where it had been decided, almost as an act of defiance, to continue Eights Week.

In order to raise an eight, the colleges agreed to amalgamate with the result that Trinity and Balliol became joined in an unlikely alliance. In fact it was almost unbelievable in view of the riot that had taken place in the Super Cinema just before the war during the showing of the film "Sanders of the River". There was a famous scene of the African war canoes paddling up the river while Paul Robeson sang the Canoe Song. On one fateful night this was greeted with a Trinity shout of "Well rowed, Balliol!" The resultant uproar became quite a notable event in the history of Trinity-Balliol battles. In those politically incorrect days it was a common joke that Balliol had a preponderance of coloured students so that one of the insults chanted by Trinity men was "Bring out your white man, Balliol." The marriage of the Master of Balliol's daughter to a Chinese gentleman was greeted with hoots of uninhibited racist glee on the Trinity side of the wall. Balliol men had equally rude things to shout at Trinity and it was all part of the good-natured feud that has spanned centuries. Now here we were as a combined eight training to uphold our colleges' place on the river. David Scrymgeour-Wedderburn of Balliol was the stroke but we used the Trinity shell, the Lady Elizabeth. At this time all the eights were housed in the OUBC boathouse on the Berkshire side of the river. As you cycled along the tow path from Folly Bridge, the rows of college barges lay along the far bank like mediaeval pavilions with their painted crests and colours and stubby flag staffs. The name Barge was a misnomer because, in fact, they were house boats which incorporated changing rooms and a furnished meeting room below the railed deck which provided a grand stand for spectators when racing was on. They wouldn't have seemed out of place on the Dahl Lake in Kashmir. Those using the changing rooms had to cross the river by the ubiquitous punt to lift their racing shells down to the river. Fifty years later I found that these attractive and decorative embellishments of the river had been replaced by a row of characterless brick sheds more suited to a suburban back yard.

How I came to be coxing this motley crew is a bit of a mystery. Cheltenham was a very minor rowing school that did all its rowing in coxed fours with no ambitions other than to try to beat Winchester at Marlowe. However all the racing on the Severn at Tewkesbury had been bumping so I had done quite a lot of it and knew a few tricks that might come in handy. The idea that anyone who is light enough can cox an eight is a popular misconception. The cox, once on the water, is master of the ship and the coaches assistant in making sure that his orders are carried out. He also has to be able to coax and encourage the crew so it helps if he knows a bit about rowing as well as being able to steer a good course. On the Isis the course is rowed upstream so the good cox will keep his boat tight under the Berkshire bank from the start until the narrow twist called the Gut where the current will take the boat gently over to the Green Bank. It has often been said that the test of a good course is that there should be leaves on the bow side oars. After this the boat has to be coaxed back to the Berkshire side by the OUBC and then more or less up the middle to the finish. Back in 1941 all the eights had long trailing rudders which were fine for washing off an opponent but had to be used very gently to avoid slowing the boat. A coxes sternest critics are his crew who don't appreciate seeing plumes of spray from an over-used rudder.

I was lucky that our coach was a splendid little man called Jock Clapperton who had been one of the University's best coxes between the wars so that I had the benefit of excellent advice such as few coxes, whose boats are coached by oarsmen, ever receive. I don't know if Jock was Trinity or Balliol or just an enthusiast but he certainly did his best for us. There is nothing more exhilarating, next to riding a galloping horse, than being pulled along a river by eight trained oarsmen. To cox an eight is therefore a great privilege and a fascinating responsibility because, in the last analysis, the cox is uniquely placed to wreck the entire enterprise. He is the only one able to ram the bank, skewer a passing skiff, or bring the boat alongside the pontoon in a manner guaranteed to remove all the rowlocks on that side. Coxes have done such things. But the price that must be paid for the pleasure is the immense pain of strict training and dieting because the cox owes it to his crew to be as light as possible.

Paddy Engelbach, having endured the agonies of getting his weight down for the Varsity boxing match, offered to supervise my training and I, rather foolishly, agreed. So every morning at 7.15 our seriously minded squad gathered at the Trinity lodge to go for a run. The crew wore a variety of light weight singlets and shorts. Paddy rather ostentatiously wore his University boxing strip and I wore three pairs of trousers and five sweaters to puff like the proverbial grampus trying to keep up. We ran down to Christ Church meadows along the bank of the river, back along the Cherwell to Magdalen Bridge and then along Holywell past New Coll to disperse at the Trinity gates. Then for the crew it was hot baths and breakfast but for the cox it was further steaming in bed with all the available blankets plus the bedside rug. For the week before Eights Week Paddy only allowed me a cup of black coffee for breakfast and a tumbler of water for the rest of the day. No alcohol of course. I managed to get down to 9 stone 4 pounds. Meanwhile the crew were slogging their way through as much meat and bread and Guiness as they could get. For additional energy they took glucose tablets before each outing.

Every afternoon we were out on the water, not only

practising ourselves but also watching the other crews with a certain amount of apprehension because we were going to start Head of the River. Bumping races are a frenetic affair. The boats start from stakes on the bank to which are tied ropes with a toggle on the end. The official rule says,"Each boat shall start from a rope held by the cox and fastened to a post on the Berkshire shore, the rope to be 50 feet in length". The distance between the starting posts was 130 feet so that on a rough calculation the boat behind, which is 60 feet long, is only about 70 feet off one's stern or just over one length. This means there is no time for one of those steadily accelerating starts which allows a rival boat to pull ahead and then overhaul it. It's flat out from the word go. To try to get a little bit of extra distance the cox leans as far back as possible holding on to the bung line. The coach crouches on the bank with a stop watch which he starts when he hears the minute gun then he counts down the last ten seconds to the start. Meanwhile the cox is trying to keep the boat straight – "touch her two", "Lightly bow" "Come forward", and then it seems as if everyone shouts "Row!"

This is the moment the cox dreads because even a slight delay in releasing the bung line can see him hoicked out of the boat like a fighter pilot ejecting. He must settle himself into his seat and concentrate on the boat ahead as well as the boat behind. What with the yells of the coaches, the cries of encouragement of the supporters, the shouting of the coxes and the splash and thump of the oars, there is general air of hysteria. With no boat ahead of me it was easy to concentrate on the boat behind which seemed to be getting inconveniently close in a very short space of time.

The two crews behind us were the combined New College/Magdalen followed by Christ Church/BNC/Pembroke with St Edmund's Hall/Queen's behind them. We reckoned that the Christ Church consortium was the fastest crew and hoped they would catch New College/Magdalen and give us a row through on the first day. We got away to a good start but the House mob failed us and, according to Jock, made a hash of their start, nearly hit the bank and almost got caught themselves. However New College/Magdalen caught

The Course

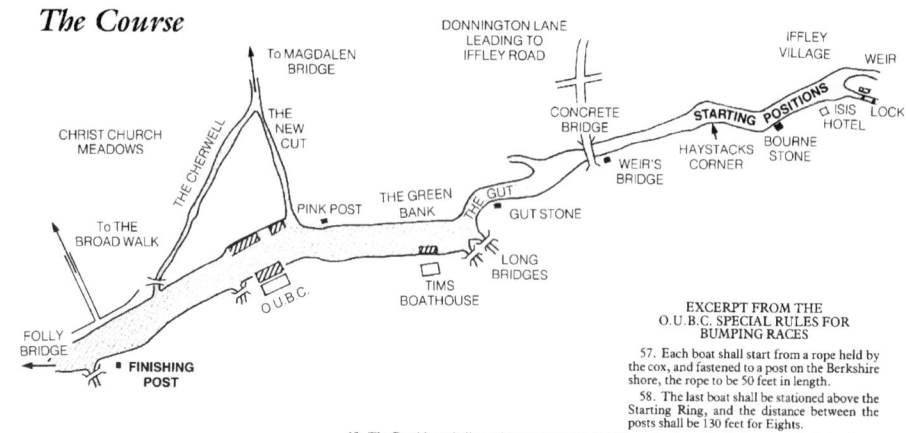

EXCERPT FROM THE O.U.B.C. SPECIAL RULES FOR BUMPING RACES

57. Each boat shall start from a rope held by the cox, and fastened to a post on the Berkshire shore, the rope to be 50 feet in length.
58. The last boat shall be stationed above the Starting Ring, and the distance between the posts shall be 130 feet for Eights.
65. The President shall provide a starter who shall fire a signal gun for the boats to take their places; after four minutes another gun; after the interval of one minute another gun for the start; after this third gun the Race shall always be held to have begun . . .
67. When a boat touches any part of the boat in front of it, or its oars or rudder, it shall be considered a bump, and also if a boat rows clean by another it shall be equivalent to a bump.
69. After every bump the boat bumping shall change places with the boat bumped whatever be their order before starting.

us just before the Gut so we were able to row round the corner and easy by the long bridges to watch with a certain grim satisfaction the House alliance being chased by Teddy Hall/ Queen's into the far distance. That was Wednesday 28th May. The next day we had our photograph taken by the Oxford Mail from the concrete bridge showing us taking a far better line approaching the Gut and closing on New College. The Christ Church cox is steering hard to avoid the bank. But we ran out of steam shortly after and were caught along the Green Bank. However that was the end of our misfortunes. For the next two days we were hotly pursued by Teddy Hall/Queen's, having to wash them off on a couple of occasions. The Oxford Mail photograph of the final day's finish shows New College/ Magdalen comfortably ahead of Christ Church/BNC/ Pembroke with Trinity/Balliol about three lengths further behind being chased past the barges in a desperate finish. Altogether we were quite pleased with our performance. It was, of course, only a small affair compared with pre and post war races. In 1939 there had been forty crews, in 1941 there were only thirteen which rowed in two divisions of six and seven crews each.

Oxford's War-time Eights: One of the close races seen yesterday. Day 2 as seen from the concrete footbrige. Oxford Mail, May 30 1941.

At the end of the Oxford Eights – New College and Magdalen finishing well in front of Christ Church, B.N.C. and Pembroke. The picturesque college barges are in the background. Keen eyes may spot our Trinity/Balliol eight in the far distance.

The scene after the race

Trinity & Balliol VIII 1941.
Back Row: D.C. Humphreys, unknown, unknown. Centre Row: W.A.O'N. Waugh, J.H. Darlington, D. Scryngeour-

Obviously there were no rewards for the rowers who had failed to stay Head of the River and rowdy celebrations such as Bumps Suppers were consigned to the annals of pre-war plenty. There was a brief bout of bread throwing and noisiness at table during Saturday night's dinner but the greatest joy for me was to be able to eat and drink normally again. We were, however, conscious of the historical significance of our alliance and posed for the traditional crew photograph but no-one seems to have noted down who we were! Years later David Humphreys identified himself as rowing Bow. Then a letter from Jim Darlington claimed that he had rowed Bow side and, being 6 foot 3, "it wouldn't have been too near the bow"! So that would put him at No 7 probably. Then I recognised Waugh and Oliphant from our Freshmen's photograph. This gives us Humphreys, Waugh, Darlington, Oliphant and Wedderburn which leaves us with at least three unsung heroes. Since we seem to have amassed four oarsman from Trinity perhaps the rest were Balliol, but Balliol have no record of their names either. It is almost inconceivable but regrettably true that it was possible for me to sit happily, day after day, in front of those eight men, to run with them each morning, to be part of that very exclusive little group that a rowing eight inevitably becomes and not to remember who they were. Even allowing that half of them were Balliol.

Celebratory drinks within College usually involved the release of tankards of College Old ale. The normal brew which we drank was the watered down wartime bitter which tradition says was once sent to the Public Analyst and received the report, "This horse is unfit for work". But College Old was a different matter. It was black and heavy and reputedly graded 5X and Cadman guarded it like gold.

"You won't get no more of that till after the war, sir, so we've got to look after it", he would say firmly while restricting us to one pint a head. If our celebrations continued after dinner it was more than likely that we would have gravitated to Ian Mollison's room across the Chapel quad. Staircase Eleven seemed to be more or less insulated as a party place, probably because of the steepness of the stairs, although Ian had been fined for throwing water and making improper use of ARP equipment (ladder broken) while "creating a disturbance on Staircase 11". But that had been in the course of end of term exuberance before Christmas. Ian had a simple method of running a party. He would place his ewer and basin on the middle of the table and pour in whatever drink anyone had brought. The resultant hell-brew could consist of whisky, gin, sherry, port, red wine and cider. In due course after the usual rounds of bawdy songs and some ritual insults shouted over the wall, Ian would produce a small bicycle and pedal furiously round the quad, finally disappearing through the Chapel arch. That usually signified the end of the party or the end of drinks. The mystery was that we never knew where he hid the bike and suspected that neither did he.

Pretty well the whole of May had been taken up with rowing and the STC, while any spare time I had was taken up by my weekly tutorial and the works of Milton on which I would be examined at the end of term. For light relief we had gone to the New Theatre to see Richard Tauber in "The Land of Smiles" in which the old show-off sang fourteen encores of "You Are My Heart's Delight" each in a different language. Mind you we had to take his word for it once he had done French and German. And still the stars kept coming. Patricia Burke, Cyril Ritchard, Leslie Henson, Binnie Hale, and Stanley Holloway in a new revue called "Up and Doing" which was having a provincial run before going in to the West End. It included two pieces which have become comedy classics, Cyril Ritchard's "Whitehall Warrior" and Stanley Holloway trying to recite "The Green Eye of the Little Yellow God" through the constant interruptions of Leslie Henson and Cyril Ritchard dressed as pukkah sahibs who knew it all.

The wonderful team of Jack Buchanan and Elsie Randolph came with a comedy-thriller called "The Body Was Well Nourished", and Mary Clare and Mary Jerrold completed their tour of "Ladies in Retirement". Then we had two weeks of D'Oyly Carte and Gilbert and Sullivan.

My brief encounter with University theatre took a distinct knock when the Experimental Theatre Club mounted a series of scenes from Shakespeare's plays in the charming setting of the Radcliffe Observatory. One of the Westfield girls called Betty Evans had persuaded Nevil and Paddy and I to do a scene from Henry the Fifth. I was supposed to be Fluellen but had completely forgotten all about it and let the others down by not knowing my lines or, for that matter, what I was supposed to be doing. I don't think Betty spoke to us after that which was sadly the end of a promising friendship.

But once the rowing was over we had time to concentrate on other things. On the evening of Thursday 5th June we crowded into the Union to hear the annual Presidential debate. It was a decorous affair with the office bearers in white tie and tails or dinner jackets. We had gone along to hear Michael Foot and R.A. Butler, neither of whom I can remember speaking, but largely we felt that this was a bit of University tradition at which we ought to be present. The group photograph in the next morning's Oxford Mail, with all the speakers and office bearers in their finery, contrasts strangely with the snippets of news that surround it; the Crete debate (the capture of Crete by German parachutists was still a matter of hot argument); 700 Suffocate in Shelter (a bomb had burst sewage and water mains above the Balham deep shelter);RAF Mess Has Art Gallery; and Tomorrow's Racing - the Coronation Cup. And even as they sat there, Hitler's forces were invading the Soviet Union, changing the whole face of the war and we, as a nation, no longer stood alone.

There was a good deal of fairly fast political footwork over this, not least from the Communists who suddenly had to convince themselves that they were really on our side after all. As an added irony the Anglo–Polish Ballet arrived at the New Theatre on 9th July led by Alicja Halama and Cjeslaw Konarski who I had seen performing the New Year's Eve Cabaret at Faletti's Hotel in Lahore only eighteen months earlier as I brought in 1940 with my parents. At that time they were refugees from the Russians as much as from the Germans.

"The Ascent of F6", which the Cherwell had lamented as lost in January, now appeared under the direction of Frank Hauser with Michael Flanders playing Shawcross and Gordon

A group at the Oxford Union presidential debate last night. Left to Right: back row, Mr H. Bird (steward), R. Gray, R.H. Jenkins (ex-librarian), R.B. McCallum, M. Kinchin-Smith, M.A. Ashcroft, G. Hersch (secretary), L. Clarke, A.E. Telling, J. Stobbs, J.A.T. Douglas (treasurer), J.G. Comyn (ex-president), K.G.I. Jones (ex-treasurer), I.J. Bahadoorsingh (ex-president). Front Row: Mr Michael Foot, Mr Richard Law, Dr G. S. Gordon (Vice-Chancellor), Mr Kenneth Riddle (president), Canon Claude Jenkins, the Rt. Hon. R.A. Butler (Under-Secretary for Foreign Affairs) and Sir George Franckenstein. Oxford Mail 6 June 1941

At New College Yesterday—a scene in the first performance of "Much Ado About Nothing," given by Friends of the Oxford University Dramatic Society. Oxford Mail 21 June 1941

*Michael Flanders in 1940 surrounded by fellow rowers
E.C.H. Warner, J.M. Coverdale, J.L. Fleure and
M.R. Wingfield*

Davies, who had been going to play the lead in "Heil Hitler", playing Ransome.

The Anglo-Polish Ballet was followed into the New by the formidable Marie Tempest in "The First Mrs Fraser". Her reputation for formidability came from Margaret Rawlings who told me that when she was in a play with Madam, she found that she could get a laugh on a certain line by moving her chair round slightly from the table at which they were supposed to be having a meal. Marie Tempest was, as usual at the head of the table facing the audience in her special spotlight. The next evening when Margaret tried to move her chair back she found that it had been screwed down on Miss Tempest's orders. No one was allowed to upstage Marie Tempest. Nevertheless she was one of the great stars of her time and once again a pleasure to watch perform.

Then the Friends of the OUDS mounted "Much Ado About Nothing" on the steps of the New College Library. This was Glynne Wickham's first production in which he gave a "creditable performance as Don John", with John Goldingham as Benedict, Michael Meyer as Dogberry, Philip Trower as Claudio, Margaret Bowden as Ursula and John Pinsent as Friar Francis. Glynne Wickham also arranged the dances with special music composed by Michael Vickers, but it was true that although the production was intelligent and the lines well spoken, "whenever Beatrice (Ann Buttrum) or Don Pedro (David Andrew) were off the stage the other players often allowed the audience's interest to flag." Diana Yeldham-Taylor did the decor and once again the ladies of the University seem to have been overlooked as it was clearly stated that the girls in the cast came from Westfield College. This played from June 20th and took advantage of the long Summer evenings to perform. Ian de Hamil was featured as Balthazar the Singer which was fortunate as his beloved Muriel Pavlow arrived at the New Theatre the following Monday in the cast of John Gielgud's production of "Dear Brutus". And what an amazing cast it had; Zena Dare, Nora Swinburne, Leon Quartermaine, Roger Livesey, Mary Jerrold, Ursula Jeans, Ronald Ward, George Howe, Gielgud himself, and Margaret Rawlings. It was a busy time for Michael Flanders too as there was ballet in the Taylorian where Sally Gilmour and Walter Gore danced to Browning's "Confessional" which was spoken by Michael.

Within the College the first tentative friendships had spread into a considerable circle. Our original foursome of Paddy, Vernon, David and me had now extended to include Derek Dawson, who had joined us on Staircase 11, Derek Bibby, David Aiers, Tony Carson, David Van Zwannenberg, Peter Balmer, Frank Margesson, Jimmy Somner, Peter Currie, Ray Peters, David Humphreys, the redoubtable Nigel Mathew and later, Byng Husband and John Boxshall. Ian Mollison moved from the confines of the Chapel quad to Staircase 13 where he succeeded in being fined once again. This time it was 30/- for breaking two window panes by throwing pebbles on June 15th. We were clearly breaking out as even Carton-Kelly, who we considered to be one of our more serious members, was fined two pounds for having a noisy party during May.

Of these, Peter Currie, Ray Peters, John Boxshall and I were to go off to war in the same regiment. Later, while in Italy, I met the good Hodgens of Fire Brigade fame under entirely different circumstances in adjacent hospital beds by Lake Trasimene. I had been blown up by a shell from one of our own guns which had fallen short and he had been blown up by a shell going off in the breech of his own 25 pounder. We discovered that it was the same gun so I can claim to be the only Trinity man to have been actually blown up by a Balliol man!

As the long vacation approached we all realised what a short acquaintance it had been. Nevil Macready and I had arranged to join the Hulbert Follies on tour but for Paddy and Vernon it was their swan song as they had completed their three term wartime degrees and were off to the RAF to train in America. I must say we envied them their future of bright lights and no rationing. We all agreed to meet in London in due course which indeed we did but it was the end of our close association.

The wartime degree was a very basic affair being designed

to be achieved in three terms, or roughly the length of deferment from the call-up that could be reasonably expected. By changing schools in my first term I had only taken two parts of the English course, Shakespeare and Milton. I still had Chaucer to negotiate but with Nevill Coghill as tutor I didn't anticipate any problem there as it was his major interest as he proved many years later by his conversion of the Canterbury Tales into the book for a long-running musical. It was one of his delights to read the Middle English aloud, emphasising the throaty guttural sounds. He also used it to drive away female students, who he didn't like, by histrionically roaring at them all the dirtiest bits. So anyway I thought that I could coast a bit during the long vacation.

The Trinity term seemed to have flashed by. So many things that we had planned to do seemed not to have been done. During the Easter vacation, Nevil and I had started to write a revue. We had visions of starting up something like the Cambridge Footlights Club which concentrated on light entertainment and had produced many leading lights in the musical theatre, not least our future employer Jack Hulbert. We even got as far as rehearsing in the Keble Common Room which by then had become the recreation room for the MI5 staff and which Pamela MacKenzie commandeered on our behalf. It was, as I remember, a typical undergraduate mixture of satire, puns and impertinence. It failed to materialise because we couldn't find anyone to play the piano for us. My only contribution was a catchy little number called the Ragtime Swing, while Nevil had penned a piece about someone falling in love with a bearded lady which started "She's hirsute, and I'm her suitor".

It was probably just as well that we abandoned it.

I am not sure when the Trinity term officially ended but as the luggage piled up at the porter's lodge waiting to be collected by the horse-drawn lorry to be taken to the station, it seemed such a short time since we had been strangers finding our way about the confusion of buildings and staircases. Clearly there were those that remained for Bolton was fined on July 17th for "breaking window pane by throwing pebbles".

Pebbles seem to have posed a constant threat to College windows. It would seem strange not having Paddy along the corridor musing on the meaning of life to "The Swan of Tuonela". David Marsh with Deanna Durbin wouldn't be quite the same.

CHAPTER TWELVE

Nevil Macready and I arrived at Reading Station on a sunny Sunday morning in July to report for duty as Assistant Stage Managers. Laurence Green, the Stage Director with the Hulbert Follies, was delighted to have us because, as he had explained when we saw him in Morecambe, there was a general shortage of back-stage crew in most of the provincial theatres and what crew there was was constantly changing because of the call-up. Most of the stage hands were enthusiastic part timers who had other jobs in the daytime. This meant that such things as mid-week matinees were often short handed. Also even those who were too old or unfit for military service were involved in various forms of shift work as air raid wardens or auxiliary firemen so that, if there was any enemy activity in the area, they had to report for duty. Sometimes a nearby army or air force camp would provide some extra personnel but again this could not be totally relied on so that before each performance there had to be an anxious head count to make sure there were enough people to work the show. So the addition of a couple of enthusiastic students to tour with the company for a few weeks was more than welcome. Our terms of service were a bit unorthodox. We were paid for each performance by the local theatre in which we worked that week and the company paid our travel expenses and something like three shillings a day because we were available during daytime at rehearsals and so on. The standard rate for stage hands was 2/6 a performance which meant that we got £1 a week for the eight performances plus 21/- from the company. Theatrical digs could be had in most towns for

25/- a week, bed and breakfast, and some of these even provided supper as well. For 35/- a week you could find quite luxurious rooms. On average this left us with about 15/- a week pocket money which we soon found we didn't have much time to spend.

Theatrical land-ladies were a very special breed. Many of them had flirted with the theatre as chorus girls or usherettes in their early days. Others were simply stage struck supporters who enjoyed having a vicarious connection with the "glamour" of the stage so that, in exchange for a modicum of gossip and an occasional free seat, there were also cups of tea or cocoa and biscuits or cake added to the daily fare. Members of the company who had been on tour before had favourite lodgings to which they always went. For the rest of us there was a list of digs pinned up on the notice board inside the stage door so that we could write or phone ahead and book for the next town. The Company Manager also travelled ahead of the show making sure that posters were up, photographs of the cast known as "frames" were in place and, as an extra favour, he would book digs for us.

But all those arrangements were ahead of us as we were greeted by George Pughe, the Stage manager. "Are you the two boys?" he asked, and from then on that's what we became the Two Boys. I don't think that Jack Hulbert, who was notoriously vague, ever worked out which of us was which.

George led us to a bay at the far end of the platform in which a long goods wagon was parked. Alongside the platform which opened onto the station yard stood a horse drawn flat railway lorry. The end of the wagon was open and we were told to dump our suitcases on the lorry and right away we were heaving big theatrical baskets which we learnt to call "skips" and assorted floods and spotlights and their stands onto the platform. A pile of scenery flats had already been loaded onto the lorry and it was obvious that it would take more than one load so, as soon as the first load was ready, we were told to accompany it to the theatre. So that was our introduction to theatrical life, clip-clopping our way, sitting side by side on the back of a railway lorry to be delivered to the Theatre Royal.

At the theatre we dumped our suitcases and joined the group of helpers which had gathered at the big doors which opened onto the street and led straight on to the empty stage. Here we met the other two back-stage members of the company, Laurence Green, who was busy telling everyone where things should go, and Harry Budd, the company stage carpenter. Both of them had been members of the Hulbert entourage for years. I had gramophone records in which Laurie Green had played in comedy sketches with Claude and Jack Hulbert. He had been Stage Director of "Under Your Hat" and was one of London's most experienced stage managers. Harry Budd, in addition to being an excellent stage carpenter and general fixer of all things that broke, was also used in cameo roles in some of the Hulbert productions. He was a tiny cheerful sparrow of a man and I remembered him being slid up and down the bar by Cicely Courtneidge in "Hide and Seek" back in 1936. Someone told me he had started life as an acrobat. In addition to them there was the local Theatre Royal stage manager who recruited the local stage hands and was, I suppose, technically our employer for the week. We looked a bit incongruous in our sports jackets, collars and ties, when all the others were in working clothes so the local SM took us in hand with our first piece of invaluable advice. "As soon as you get in the theatre, even if you're not going to do anything, take off your jackets".

When the first load had been disposed of, the lorry went clattering back to the station and Laurie told us to go and find our digs. We collected the address from the stage door keeper and staggered off with our suitcases. If we had had thoughts of a taxi it wouldn't have been much use in Reading on a Sunday afternoon in wartime. In due course we found ourselves in a grim back street. On one side was a row of little red brick houses and on the other the huge red brick wall of the Huntley and Palmer biscuit factory. We were received by a friendly woman in an overall who showed us to our room. For cheapness we had agreed to share but hadn't expected to be confronted by a big old fashioned iron double bedstead. However it was clean if basic but there were other setbacks. The house had no bathroom, the only washing facility being a brass cold water tap over the sink in the kitchen down stairs. Hot water had to be heated in kettles on the gas stove. I suppose that for 21/- a week bed and breakfast we shouldn't have expected more and, in a way, it was no more basic than an Oxford college. Our chief subsequent shock came when we woke up next morning and found that the feather mattress had piled up between us in the middle of the bed and we were virtually lying on the springs. In fact when I awoke I could see noone else in the bed and assumed that Nevil had already got up to shave. He had assumed the same thing, so that when we both sat up and found the other there it was so like Laurel and Hardy that we collapsed laughing. But there was hot tea to revive us and an adequate breakfast to set us up for the morning's work.

We arrived at the theatre at ten o'clock to find that the back stage crew had been there since eight and that ten was the call time for the cast. So that was lesson number two. We swiftly applied lesson number one and took off our jackets and hung them on the nearest convenient nail. Then we learnt lesson number three which was how to tie a clove hitch. We were then initiated into the multitude of mysteries with which we would become familiar in the following weeks. Every theatre has a space above the stage where the scenery, backcloths and so on are hung or flown - therefore called the Flies. A gantry about the height of the proscenium arch above the stage was called the Fly Floor. The scenery was hauled up or let down with ropes which were tied off on cleats on the fly floor. The scenery was hung from a batten or had a batten built into it. Down on the stage we were shown how to tie the three ropes that hung down from the flies onto the battens. The rope furthest away from the gantry was called the Long, then there was the Middle and the Short. As each cloth was ready for flying, Laurie Green, sitting in the stalls would check it for level. "Up on your long. Down on your short a bit. Hold it there. Tie off at that", and on the fly floor each set of ropes would be secured and marked. In one theatre we worked a few weeks later the fly man had already hung and tied off the cloths before Laurie arrived. As they went through the ritual of "Up on your Long, down on your short" and so on, the fly man merely plucked the ropes so that the cloth bounced a little. When Laurie appeared to be satisfied the fly man turned to me and said "He can't tell me how to hang a bloody cloth!" So we learnt to call the curtains that formed the wings Legs, and the curtains that pulled across Tabs - short for Tableaux Curtains no less. The little trap doors on either side of the stage which held the plugs for floods and spots that were stood in the wings we called Dips and, of course. the footlights across the front of the stage were Floats, so called because in the days before electricity the lighting was provided by wicks floating in oil. Which probably explains why so many theatres burnt down. And while all these things were being sorted out, costumes hung in the dressing rooms, props placed in their strategic positions, the first agonised noises from the orchestra pit indicated that the local band was having its first run through the musical score.

By mid-day everything had been plugged in, tied off, checked and made ready for the lighting rehearsal. This involved Laurie Green walking through all the movements of the show and telling the electricians what was required according to the cue sheet. Jack Hulbert was a lighting fanatic. All his shows had complicated and imaginative lighting plots which were enough to test the permanent crew of a West End theatre. In the Hulbert Follies there were some three hundred lighting cues in the two and a half hour show. Many of these were quick black-outs at the end of short sketches which meant that the operators of the front arcs had literally to be spot on. This presented a problem as most theatres of the day had only very embryonic communication systems consisting of a wind-up field telephone sort of thing or, more likely, a simple set of red and green lights for Stand By and Go.

Trying to follow the action on stage, and listen or watch for a cue while keeping an eye on the cue sheet was an almost impossible task as, in most cases, the first time that the operators had seen the full show was on the first night on Monday. So, in the end, the only solution was for one of the company to go up into the box in the roof of the theatre to cue the lights personally. Now they had the Two Boys and I found myself detailed to climb up to the Gods and then a bit higher to join the spotlight operators in their hot little projection box. That became my regular Monday night chore. In addition I quickly had to learn how to operate the carbon arc myself because when the Wednesday matinee came round one of the operators failed to turn up.

Meanwhile Nevil remained down on the stage where he had switched his allegiance from the pretty young Renna to the even prettier and more glamourous Jean Gillie, a well known film starlet with the additional aura of having been Jack Buchanan's mistress. But on the Monday night no-one was spotted with more care and devotion than Cynthia as she leapt on from the upstage wing to open the show. So our first night seemed to pass off without disaster and we were able to get a complete look at the company we had joined. It was very much a family show. Jack Hulbert and Cicely Courtneidge, their daughter Pamela, recruited rather against her will, Claude Hulbert who had his wife Enid with him, Myrette Morven who was Cicely's understudy, and Fred Kitchen Junior who was Jack's. Fred, who came from a well known theatrical family, and Myrette played in their own right in the sketches and routines of the show together with a splendid old time actor called Henry "Tommy" Thompson. Jean Gillie was the song and dance juvenile - the role they used to call the Soubrette. Claude's wife had also performed in earlier shows as Enid Trevor so that, at a pinch, she could understudy Myrette Morven. Then there were the girls. Iris Tully, Eunice Crowther, Peggy Watson, Renna Caste, Sabina Gordon, Doreen Arden, Betty Martin, Pamela Shepherd and Gola James, who was Laurie Green's wife, had all been in Hulbert's hand picked chorus for "Under Your Hat". For the Follies they were joined by George Pughe's wife Mickie Decima, who was Hy Hazell's sister, a beautiful girl called Hermione Moir and my lovely Cynthia. Back stage there was Laurie Green, George Pughe,

Harry Budd, Mrs Doughty, the wardrobe mistress, and we two dogsbodies. Cis Courtneidge had a dresser called Helen and Jack's dresser was also the chauffeur of his Rolls Royce. The Musical Director was Bob Probst, who led from the piano and a second pianist whose name I forget who played for rehearsals. Lionel Monte was the lead violinist and Len Hunt the drummer, later to be replaced by Harry Barker. This meant that the show could be worked in some places by two pianos and drums and, in view of the strange noises that sometimes emanated from the orchestra pit, this might have been better. But when one thinks of it, for all these provincial theatres to manage to raise an orchestra was something of an achievement. All the young musicians were in the services so that, for the most part, the local bands consisted of the elderly or infirm or enthusiastic amateurs. Some towns, like Oxford, had nearby military establishments where bandsmen were sometimes available. The London orchestras relied heavily on the Brigade of Guards, so much so that at one time the Welsh were referred to as the Geraldo Guards. In fact the Reading band wasn't too bad and the only really dodgy one was in Derby where Lionel Monte asked the local violinist to sound his A and was asked "Why?". Later on Jean Gillie left and was replaced by a reluctant Pamela Hulbert, and Fred Kitchen gave way to a young Terence Alexander making his first professional appearance.

Nevil's faithful squiring of Jean Gillie received a set back when a well groomed and smartly dressed RAF officer called for her at the stage door. The stage door keeper gave me the message, "Tell Miss Gillie that Squadron Leader Profumo is here to see her". And it was so. The final blow to his hopes and esteem came when she asked him to send a telegram on her behalf to Mr Profumo arranging to meet him in London and signed "Tiddles."

But it was beautiful weather and the early evening show time meant that we could hire a couple of punts on the Thames and have a romantic supper by moonlight on the river. This idyllic weather continued when we moved on to Bath to play in the lovely little Theatre Royal where the cobblestones of the original groundlings could be seen under the floor of the stalls and where we had to do some urgent alterations to our sets to enable them to fit the stage. There we spent all our spare time swimming in the river or floating in the sulphrous waters of the Roman baths.

The routine of touring was soon learnt and on Saturday nights we packed everything away in the skips as soon as they were finished with so that by the time the curtain came down it didn't take more than an hour to roll up the cloths, fold the tabs and legs and pack up the lights. The lorry waited outside the scene dock and the railway wagon was ready in its bay waiting to be loaded ready to be attached to the train the next morning.

On tour with the Hulbert Follies, me bathing at Bath

Train call was usually around ten o'clock when the company would get into its reserved carriage to be taken to the next town. This general post of theatrical companies took place all over Britain every Sunday and must have posed the most enormous logistical problems but because civilian morale was considered to be so important, the entertainment industry had special concessions and priorities to enable shows to be mounted and toured. Performers could be reserved and kept out of the services as long as they were working. In exchange they had to do a certain amount of war work. The chorus girls, when in London, reported once a week to a factory in Victoria to tie camouflage nets. Jack Hulbert had joined the police reserve after playing a policeman in "Jack's The Boy". Every Saturday night after the show he used to be driven to London to do an eight hour shift on the beat or, as he became more senior, in the police station. Claude Hulbert was in the Auxiliary Fire Brigade. Cicely Courtneidge had adopted the men who manned the lonely anti-aircraft gun and balloon barrage sites. These were small units often miles from anywhere. Every Sunday she used to take Bob Probst and a couple of the girls to put on a show for them and, in the interval at the theatre, she used to appeal for comforts for these often forgotten small units. We put a couple of skips in the foyer to collect donations. Someone even turned up with a piano!

In some places the company had to book into accommodation quite a long way from the theatre because of the air raids. In Cardiff, where we played the Prince of Wales Theatre, we were billeted out at Barry along the coast and had to come in each day by train. One evening, because of an air raid warning, the train carrying the cast stopped in a tunnel and we had to keep the audience happy for nearly forty minutes while we telephoned desperately to find out where they were. In Brighton we played the Hippodrome, a magnificently equipped theatre with its own power plant. This caused one problem in that the lights were so bright that you couldn't see across the stage into the opposite wings so that our usual hand signals to change colours in the floods were useless. Nevertheless the theatre was fully staffed even to a call boy in a Buttons uniform. The days of having loud speakers in every dressing room relaying the show were still far off so the call boy, or girl, was an important cog in the machine making sure that everyone was called in time for their cue. The young lad in Brighton was not only smart but cheeky. When Laurie Green ticked him off for some misdemeanour he looked him straight in the eye and said, "Next week, Mister, you'll just be a memory to me". It was here that we survived a minor crisis. Jack was a perfectionist and preferred a very relaxed style of dancing. Poor Cynthia fell into disfavour because he felt that she overworked so he was prompted by Laurie to replace her with Laurie's wife in the opening ballet. Cynthia came to me in floods of tears because her parents were coming down to Brighton to see the show. But Jack was a kind man and when he was told this Cynthia was reinstated to her little moment of solo glory.

We were booked in to a block of flats on the sea front called Ross Mansions. Across the road was the beach with a huge barbed wire entanglement running along it. We were told that the beach was also mined. The famous pier had a section removed at the landward end to prevent any adventurous Germans from getting ashore by climbing on to it. It seemed strange that here we were on the invasion coast. If we were to be invaded this might be where they would land. Did the Germans mount commando raids? If they did or if they had invaded, the first thing they would have encountered would have been a troup of chorus girls and some assorted hangers on. I suppose that might have held them up until help arrived.

But the sun shone and the sea glistened and the only shock anyone had was when one of the girls knocked a milk bottle off the window sill and it landed like a small bomb near an elderly lady who was walking her dog. The only sounds of battle we heard was when we went to see Anton Walbrook in "Dangerous Moonlight" and came home humming the Warsaw Concerto. It must have been the craziest and quietest front line in history.

Margaret came down from London to see us and to see if someone could help her with a problem. In March of 1941, the call-up had been extended to cover everyone, male and female, from eighteen to fifty-five. This meant that Margaret might find herself drafted into the services or, worse, into a factory. The reliable Len Hunt came speedily to the rescue. His friend Gerald Bright, better known as Geraldo, was musical director of the Entertainment National Service Association - ENSA. He was sure that he could find Margaret a job in the organisation whose Headquarters were in Drury Lane Theatre. In due course she was introduced to Roger Ould, who was head of the radio division, and as Nevil and I headed off for Birmingham with the company, Margaret reported for duty to Drury Lane as a studio secretary.

The Theatre Royal in Birmingham was one of the Moss Empire chain and, like the Brighton Hippodrome, had an excellent staff. There were three front arcs operated by men smartly dressed in white boiler suits. It made me feel inordinately scruffy. The arcs were housed in a box that was actually outside the dome of the theatre and once it became dark and they were blacked out it was like the Black Hole of Calcutta. So much so that the operators took off their boiler suits and worked in their underpants and you could see the waves of tobacco smoke from the audience swirling up the beam of the arc to be trapped in the sweat box. The local health authority had prescribed a pint of fresh milk a day to compensate for the discomfort. There were still air raids on Birmingham and the Midlands and I remember hoping that one wouldn't happen while the show was on as our perch outside the roof seemed a bit exposed. I must confess that I kept an eye on that little green light shining beside the proscenium.

When we got to the Opera House, Manchester, we could see the battering the city had taken and the company had to stay out at Wilmslow in the Southern suburbs. Here we had the misfortune to clash with "Up and Doing". Our show had been to Manchester before and on the Wednesday matinee we played to thirty-six people in an auditorium that seats about two thousand. Once we had found them, we put them all together in the stalls and went throught the pass door to join them and applaud the acts. It was one of the best shows the cast ever gave!

Memories of theatrical touring in wartime are necesarily kaleidescopic. Walking down Snow Hill tunnel in Birmingham to look for our scene truck and then persuading an engine driver to shunt it into the loading bay. In Derby, arriving at the theatre and being about to crash in when we realised that there was an orchestra on the stage and we were getting a very dirty look from the conductor. It was Malcolm Sargent

ACT I.
1. OPENING—THE FOLLIES.
2. INCREDIBLE HAPPENINGS (Ronald Jeans) . . . THE COMPANY
3. SWEET SIXTEEN (Jack Yellen and Ray Henderson). JEAN GILLIE and CHORUS
4. THE MATCHMAKER (Ronald Jeans).
   John . . . . JACK HULBERT
   Charles . . . . CLAUDE HULBERT
   Stella . . . . PAMELA ROSEMARY
   Mary (John's Wife) . . . . JEAN GILLIE
5. THE SOUTH IS THE PLACE FOR ME . CICELY COURTNEIDGE and FOLLY GIRLS
6. JACK and CLAUDE HULBERT.
7. ROOM 504 (Eric Maschwitz and George Posford).
   The Girl . . . . JEAN GILLIE   The Husband . . BRIAN HILL
   The Wife . PAMELA ROSEMARY   The Boots . . FRED KITCHEN
            SCENE . . . . A Hotel Corridor.
8. GREEK AS SHE IS TAUGHT (Ronald Jeans).
   The Schoolmaster . . . . JACK HULBERT
   The Boy . . . . CICELY COURTNEIDGE
            SCENE . . . A Classroom.
9. FINALE—THE FOLLIES.
   (a) Ridin' High . . . . JACK HULBERT
   (b) Loving You (Claude Hulbert) . . . . JACK and CLAUDE HULBERT
   (c) Lady Needs a Change (Dorothy Fields and Arthur Schwartz)
                                          CICELY COURTNEIDGE
   (d) We Three . . . . CICELY COURTNEIDGE
   (e) Let's Have Another One (Don Raye and Hughie Prince) JACK HULBERT
   (f) . . . . THE FOLLIES

ACT II.
1. OPENING—THE FOLLIES.
2. THE GREAT WHITE SALE (Dion Titheradge).
   Mrs Spoone   CICELY COURTNEIDGE
   Shop Assistant . . . . CLAUDE HULBERT
   Shop Walker . . . . HENRY THOMPSON
            SCENE . Harridges Drapery Department.
3. HOW BRITAIN FIGHTS (Eric Maschwitz).
   Comperes . . LAURENCE GREEN and FRED KITCHEN
   Bus Driver . . . . HENRY THOMPSON
   Typist . . . . PAMELA ROSEMARY
   Jim Crow . . . . CLAUDE HULBERT
   Mum . . . . CICELY COURTNEIDGE
   Dad . . . . JACK HULBERT
4. RHYTHM. . . . . Misses CROWTHER, WATSON and MARTIN
5. BUTTERFLY ON THE WHEEL (Ronald Jeans).
   Richard Grayson . . . . JACK HULBERT
   Iris B. Carstairs . . . . JEAN GILLIE
   A.A. Solicitor . . . . HENRY THOMPSON
   P.C. Buffy . . . . FRED KITCHEN
   Magistrate . . . . BRIAN HILL
   Clerk of the Court . . . . CHARLES FITZMAURICE
   Prosecuting Solicitor . . . . LAURENCE GREEN
            SCENE . A Provincial Police Court.
6. TEXAS JOE (Claude Hulbert). . . . CLAUDE HULBERT
7. VELVEETA HAS A LINE (Ronald Jeans).
   George . . . . BRIAN HILL
   Henry . . . . JACK HULBERT
   Velveeta . . . . CICELY COURTNEIDGE

The Hulbert Follies programme when they first played Manchester in 1941.

8. JACK HULBERT.
9. THE DOWAGER FAIRY QUEEN (Douglas Furber and Ivor Novello).
   Principal Boy . . . . PAMELA ROSEMARY
   Principal Girl . . . . CYNTHIA CLIFFORD
   Demon King . . . . HENRY THOMPSON
   Witch . . . . FRED KITCHEN
   Fairy Queen . . . . CICELY COURTNEIDGE
10. DRAKE (Words and Music by Claude Hulbert)
   CLAUDE HULBERT and HENRY THOMPSON
11. LOVE'S RE-AWAKENING (Ronald Jeans).
   Mr. Padge . . . BRIAN HILL   Henry Pullet . JACK HULBERT
   Agnes . . PAMELA ROSEMARY .Clara Pullet . CICELY COURTNEIDGE
        SCENE . The Parlour behind Henry Pullet's Leather Shop.
12. FINALE—THE FOLLIES.

Produced by JACK HULBERT.

Dances arranged by Jack Hulbert and Philip Buchel.   Musical Director, Robert Probst.
Miss Courtneidge's frock designed and executed by Strassner.
Girls' costumes designed by Strassner and executed by B. J. Simmons.
Men's costume by Morris Angel.   Shoes by Raynes.   Wigs by Nathanwigs.   Cigarettes by Abdulla.
Stage Director - LAURENCE GREEN. Stage Manager - GEORGE PUGHE. Business Manager - GEORGE HARRIS.

MONDAY, 28th APRIL, FOR SIX NIGHTS AT 6.
Matinees : Wednesday and Saturday at 2.

JACK BUCHANAN
in **THE BODY WAS WELL NOURISHED,** with
ELSIE RANDOLPH

To **STAMP COLLECTORS**
We carry a stock of over half a million stamps to suit every type of collector. Approvals against references.

DUPLICATES LTD.
4 WOOD STREET, DEANSGATE
(Opposite Finnigans)   Tel. BLA 5747-8

Table **J&B** Waters
SUPPLIED TO THIS THEATRE

By Appointment
to the late King George V
JEWSBURY & BROWN Ltd.

WHICH PIANO?

When the question is raised, the answer should be: the Instrument which has won a reputation for "Quality" and held that reputation.

THE CRANE PIANO

has been the choice of the professional musician, teacher and student for upwards of a century. In respect to excellence of craftsmanship, the Crane Piano has few rivals, for it is built to give a lifetime's service, whilst tonal qualities will please the most exacting critic. Prices are very moderate, from 27 guineas, and purchase terms are arranged to suit your convenience.

May we send you our 1941 Catalogue ?

Crane & Sons Lt.
202-204 DEANSGATE   MANCHESTER

The Hulbert Follies programme when they first played Manchester in 1941.

Cynthia–make & mend in the chorus dressing room.

and the London Philharmonic. Here Nevil and I were thrown out of our digs because we complained that the sheets had obviously been used before. "It was good enough for Evelyn Laye, so it's good enough for you. Get out!". So out we got and were sitting disconsolately on our suitcases when a soldier heading home on leave found us and took us home. His parents took the arrival of a couple of extra chaps in their stride, bunked us in for the night and saw us off with breakfast in the morning to find new digs. Derby had a strange atmosphere caused by the incessant smoke. Because it was the home of the Rolls Royce factory, huge stoves were placed around the town in which some chemical concoction was burnt to keep the place under an almost permanent smoke screen. Added to this my operation of the front arc wasn't improved by being told that my predecessor had electrocuted himself on it.

Reading, Bath, Cardiff, Brighton, Birmingham, Manchester, Derby and Northampton, sixty-four performances, eight get-ins and get-outs was the total of our experience but, when we left the show after Northampton, we felt that we were now fully fledged professionals. We had certainly worked with some of the best people in the business and made friends that would last us the rest of our lives. It was a sad parting but when we got to London we found that Len Hunt had organised a box for us at the London Palladium for the Jazz Jamboree which he had helped to organise in his capacity of Vice-Chairman of the Musicians Social and Benevolent Council. For Margaret this was an initiation into the world of dance bands and musicians which would fill her life for the next five years. It was a huge production featuring twelve bands and every top musician in Britain. The comperes were Sam Browne, a leading vocalist of his day, and Christopher Stone and David Miller, who were well known presenters of popular music on the BBC before the term "Disc Jockey" had been invented. It was 7th September 1941.

Freddie Bretherton and the resident Palladium orchestra opened the proceedings with a standard "on with the show" type of medley and then the opening band on stage was Joe Loss and his Orchestra using their new hit arrangement of "In The Mood" as their signature tune instead of "Dancing Time." It was, in fact, the famous Glenn Miller version almost note for note but none of us had heard it then. The show was being broadcast and the first sensation came when vocalist Bob Arden strode onto the stage confidently starting his number in the wrong key. "Come on, Bob, I know you're just kidding", said Mr Loss with the sort of smile that alligators are supposed to have and they started again. After they had gone through their repertoire featuring a battery of vocalists including Chick Henderson's "Begin The Beguine", we realised that this was certainly a Jamboree but Jazz it was not. However, next came the great RAF Dance Band, The Squadronaires, with a swinging Bob Crosby style version of "South Rampart Street Parade", a new WAAF vocalist called Doreen Lundy singing "Dolores" and an outstanding version of Gene Krupa's "Drummin' Man" with Tommy McQuater on trumpet and Jock Cummings on drums which we thought was better than the original. George Evans, one of the key members of the Geraldo orchestra had an all-saxophone group called Saxes 'n Sevens which worked at the Embassy Club and had some interesting harmonies but had a typical night club blandness. Then a new Latin-American band led by Edmundo Ros made its debut straggling on to the stage looking, as David Miller said, like an animated bus queue. Max Bacon presented the Feldman Trio consisting of Robert Feldman on clarinet, Monty Feldman on accordion and a miniscule, seven-year-old Victor Feldman pounding his drums in an excerpt from Artie Shaw's "Concerto for Clarinet". That was a show stopper and was followed by Johnny Claes and his Claepigeons who provided some of the only real jazz of the afternoon and certainly featured the best jazz singer in Benny Lee. They were followed by the next of the three service bands from No.1 Balloon Centre led by Paul Fenhoulet. Paul, leading the band as a trombonist, had chosen a more Tommy Dorsey style of swing but there was great argument as to whether his rhythm section of Pat Dodd (piano), Jack Cooper (guitar), Jock Reid (bass) and Jock Jacobsen (drums) wasn't better than the Squadronaire's Ronnie Aldrich (piano), Sid Colin (guitar), Arthur Maden (bass) and Jock Cummings (drums). Harry Parry and his Rhythm Club Sextet featured George Shearing on piano, Roy Marsh doing a Lionel Hampton on vibraphone and Geraldo's pretty vocalist Doreen Villiers. The Army was represented by Eric Tann and the Blue Rockets RAOC Dance Orchestra. Then there was an emotional moment when the curtains opened to reveal the survivors of the Ken Johnson Orchestra, some still in splints and bandages, playing without a conductor, a single spot marking the place where Ken would have stood if he had not been killed when the Cafe de Paris had been bombed a few months earlier.

So it was a swing rather than a Jazz Jamboree and it was brought to a close by the augmented Geraldo Orchestra, a sixteen strong chorus, soprano Olive Groves and Arthur Young at the piano performing a sort of concerto á la Warsaw he had written called "Song of Freedom". Rather pretentious, very spectacular and certainly not jazz! However it was a most successful afternoon and as a showcase for British dance bands it was excellent even if it was derivative.

"JAZZ JAMBOREE, 1941"

SUNDAY, 7th SEPTEMBER
LONDON PALLADIUM

THE COMPERES:

SAM BROWNE   CHRISTOPHER STONE   DAVID MILLER

Overture:

FREDDIE BRETHERTON AND THE PALLADIUM ORCHESTRA

Violins: W. B. RICHARDSON (leader)
C. VERNE
A. JAMES
H. PETTS
R. JORRE
F. BILBE

Violas: N. E. EVANS
M. GOMEZ

Cellos: J. SOWERBY
J. SIGALL

Bass: A. COUSINS
Piano: C. BAMPTON
Flute: L. HOLMES
Oboe: J. FIELD
Clarinets: S. FELL
R. THOMPSON

Bassoon: M. PORT
Trumpets: V. ELLIOT
S. WRIGHT
G. REGAN
R. WALTON

Trombones: D. JOHN
S. KNIGHT
Percussion: R. F. FLOWER

EDMUNDO ROS AND HIS RUMBA BAND

EDMUNDO ROS
LESLIE THOMPSON
ROBERTO INGLEZ
SANTIAGO LOPEZ
RAY ELGAR
FRANK DENIZ
DENNIS WALTON

THE FELDMAN TRIO

Presented by MAX BACON

Clarinet and Saxophone: ROBERT FELDMAN
Accordion: MONTY FELDMAN
Drums: VICTOR FELDMAN

JOE LOSS AND HIS BAND

Saxes: REG BREWSTER
WALTER CROMBIE
TOMMY FIELDS
NORMAN IMPEY
DANNY MILLER

Trumpets: HARRY LETHAM
BILL BURTON
STAN STANTON

Trombones: BILL BOLAND
DON MACAFFER

Piano: ALBERT GORDON
Guitar: JOE YOUNG
Bass: SYD BURKE
Percussion: JACK GREENWOOD
Vocalists: BETTE ROBERTS
IRENE JOHNSON
CHICK HENDERSON
BOB ARDEN
DON RIVUS

THE KEN JOHNSON ORCHESTRA
(Reformed by CARL BARRITEAU)

Saxes: CARL BARRITEAU
GEORGE ROBERTS
AUBREY FRANKS
BILLY AMSTELL

Trumpets: LESLIE HUTCHISON
DAVID WILKINS
KEN BAKER

Trombones: FREDDY BUTT
LADDIE BUSBY

Piano: YORKE DE SOUZA
Guitar: JOE DENIZ
Bass: TOM BROMLEY
Drums: TOM WILSON
Vocalist: DON JOHNSON

HARRY PARRY AND HIS RHYTHM CLUB SEXTET
With DOREEN VILLIERS

Clarinet: HARRY PARRY
Solo Electric Guitar: LAUDERIC CAYTON
Spanish Guitar: FRANK DENIZ
Piano: GEORGE SHEARING
Drums: BEN EDWARDS
Bass: CHARLES SHORT
Vibraphone: ROY MARSH

GERALDO
and his
(Augmented)
CONCERT ORCHESTRA

Soloist: OLIVE GROVES
CHORUS OF SIXTEEN
Solo Piano: ARTHUR YOUNG

Oboe:	T. JONES
Clarinet:	BERNARD WALTON
Bassoon:	T. WIGHTMAN
1st Alto Saxophone:	HARRY HAYES ✓
2nd Alto Saxophone:	NAT TEMPLE ✓
1st Tenor Saxophone:	GEORGE EVANS ✓
2nd Tenor Saxophone:	ARTHUR BIRKBY ✓
1st Trumpet:	ALFIE NOAKES ✓
2nd Trumpet:	RONNIE PRIEST ✓
3rd Trumpet:	GEORGE RATCLIFFE ✓
1st Trombone:	TED HEATH ✓
2nd Trombone:	JIMMY COOMBS ✓
3rd Trombone:	JOE FERRIE ✓
Horns:	E. SELLERS / F. HAMILTON
Harp:	MARIE KORCHINSKA
Piano:	SID BRIGHT ✓
Tuba:	W. BELL
Percussion:	JACK SIMPSON / MAURICE BURMAN ✓

"SAXES 'N SEVENS"
PRESENTED BY
ANGLO AMERICAN ARTISTES LTD.
With GEORGE EVANS
FROM
THE EMBASSY CLUB, W.1

Altos:	HARRY HAYES / LES GILBERT / NORMAN MALONEY
Solo Tenor:	GEORGE EVANS
Tenors:	AUBREY FRANKS / FRANK MELLOR / TONY MERVYN
Piano:	RONNIE SELBY
Guitar:	JOE DENIZ
Bass:	WILKIE DAVIDSON
Drums:	BOBBY MIDGELEY

Violins:	MAURICE LINDON / CHARLES KATZ / W. MONRO / H. AYCKBOURNE / I. LOSOWSKY / T. JONES / E. ROLOFF / N. COMRAS / M. GUYLER / J. KUCHMY / R. WORRALL / W. MERNICK / F. BILBE / B. LEWIS / D. NACHMANSON / HARRY SHERMAN
Violas:	JOHN DENMAN / J. LOCKIER / N. BIRNBAUM / LAURIE DAVIES
Cellos:	JAMES WHITEHEAD / GEORGE ROTH / FRANK WALKER / G. WILLIAMS / M. COLLINS
Basses:	JACK COLLIER / SAM MOLYNEUX / JOCK REID / DON STUTELEY
Flutes:	PAT EYDEMANN / PHIL GOODY

THE DANCE ORCHESTRA OF H.M. ROYAL AIR FORCE
(By permission of Air Council)
"THE SQUADRONAIRES"
Leader, Vocalist: SGT. JIMMY MILLER

Altos:	L.A.C. TOMMY BRADBURY / L.A.C. HARRY LEWIS	Trombones:	L.A.C. ERIC BREEZE / L.A.C. GEORGE CHISHOLM
Tenors:	L.A.C. ANDY McDEVITT / L.A.C. JIMMY DURRANT	Guitar:	L.A.C. SID COLIN
		Piano:	L.A.C. RONNIE ALDRICH
		Bass:	L.A.C. ARTHUR MADEN
Trumpets:	CPL. TOMMY McQUATER / L.A.C. ARCHIE CRAIG	Drums:	L.A.C. JOCK CUMMINGS
		Vocalist:	L.A.C. BILLY NICHOLLS

No. 1 BALLOON CENTRE DANCE ORCHESTRA
A Band of H.M. Royal Air Force
(By kind permission of Group Captain K. F. Argus, O.B.E., M.C., T.D.)

Leader:	PAUL FENHOULET	3rd Trumpet:	TED ALLABY
1st Alto:	ISSY DUMAN	1st Trombone:	PAUL FENHOULET
2nd Alto:	BILL APPS	2nd Trombone:	GEORGE THORNE
1st Tenor:	CLIFF TIMMS	Guitar:	JACK COOPER
2nd Tenor:	BASIL SKINNER	Piano:	PAT DODD
1st Trumpet:	CHICK SMITH	Bass:	JOCK REID
2nd Trumpet:	LES LAMBERT	Drums:	JOCK JACOBSEN

R.A.O.C. "BLUE ROCKETS" DANCE ORCHESTRA
Directed by L.Cpl. ERIC TANN
(By kind permission of Brig. E. P. Readman, O.B.E., T.D.)

Violins:	ERIC ROBINSON / ERIC HARRINGTON
Saxophones:	GEORGE CLOUSTON / VICTOR KNIGHT / BERNIE DANIELS / SHIRLEY WALDRON
Trumpets:	GEORGE HAWKINS / TOMMY KEITH / HARRY COCKER
Trombones:	ERIC TANN / RONNIE RAND / SAM GELSLEY
Guitar:	JACK BAVERSTOCK
Piano:	
Bass and Vocalist:	ERIC WHITLEY
Drums:	LEW STEVENSON
Compere and Dancer:	LEE STREET

JOHNNY CLAES AND HIS CLAEPIGEONS

Solo Flute:	GEOFFREY GILBERT
1st Alto:	HARRY HAYES
2nd Alto:	GERRY ALVAREZ
3rd Alto:	GEORGE HARRISON
1st Tenor:	ANDY McDEVITT
2nd Tenor:	AUBREY FRANKS
Piano:	TOMMY POLLARD
Bass:	CHARLIE SHORT
Guitar:	IVOR MAIRANTS
Drums:	CARLO KRAHMER
Vocalist:	BENNY LEE

It was indicative of the total mastery of the air that the RAF had already achieved that a show such as this could be mounted in the heart of London. The Americans were still safely neutral, the Russians being driven inexorably back to the Leningrad-Moscow line, the disasters of Greece and Crete had taken place and we were being chased out of Libya back into Egypt again, yet there was an air of totally unaccountable confidence in the future. The Jazz Jamboree seemed to epitomise this extraordinary feeling.

CHAPTER THIRTEEN

Returning to Trinity after the long vacation was like coming home. My rooms were filled with familiar things, Persian rugs from Mull on the floor, a couple of favourite reproductions on the wall - Anna Zinkeisen and inevitably Degas-, a lot of books not all dictated by the English course, my old blue eiderdown on the bed, a tartan rug thrown over the settee, my Leedy snare drum in the corner and some papers where I had left them on the desk. My faithful portable HMV gramophone stood on the side of the desk with its pile of records beside it and my small bakelite wireless set was on its little table in the corner. North was bustling about helping new arrivals into their rooms and I could hear his standard litany being recited. Only a year before I had been the new boy anxiously absorbing the college routines. Now I was no longer a freshman but, by wartime standards, a comparatively old hand. The staircase had a lot of new faces, in fact only three of us, Derek Dawson, Derek Bibby and I were inhabitants from the Trinity term. As well as the influx of freshers there had been a sort of general post of residents. David Marsh had moved into rather grand rooms on Staircase 16. Williams and Shoeten-Sack had moved in from somewhere and Byng Husband from Staircase 9. We were joined by Messrs Gray, Robertson, Armstrong, Hodgson, and Parrington. I wondered if they regarded us with the same awe as we had our predecessors a year before when we attended our first JCR meeting.

Whatever air of superiority we might have wished to assume was rather spoilt by the admission of the JCR President that he couldn't find the minutes of the previous meeting so he couldn't ask the Secretary to read them. Unfortunately the minutes of this first meeting of the term do not name the President but by a process of elimination it looks as if it might have been Duncan Davies. Jimmy Somner was elected Secretary and thereafter the following elections were made:-

> Mr M.E. Lock as Captain of Rugger with Mr Mitchell as Secretary.
> Mr Martin as Captain of Squash,
> Mr Dawson as Captain of Soccer,
> Mr Partridge as Captain of Hockey with Mr Bowdler as Secretary.

The food committee must have worked satisfactorily because the same team of Messrs Martin, Bolton, Reinhold and Somner was re-elected with the rather ominous proviso that they would be expected to report on their activities to the next JCR meeting.

Mr Locke, E.M. presumably, was elected Master of the Rolls, I became Rear Admiral and Roger Hammick was "unanimously elected Garden Boy."

There had obviously been a problem with bicycles being taken from the cellar. It was pointed out that the only way to avoid having one's bicycle pinched was to padlock the wheels effectively. I had found that trying to stop people from pinching one's bike was so time consuming that it was easier to walk to most places and I only used my bike to go down to the river and along the tow path. Most colleges made you park your bike outside which meant that, if you arrived early to attend a lecture, your bike speedily disappeared under a pile of other bikes so that if you wanted to sneak off early you couldn't get to it. Confronted by this situation, there were those with fewer scruples who solved it by taking the first available unlocked bike off the pile thus starting a chain reaction of bike borrowing. One way of discouraging this was to paint your bike in some clearly identifiable manner so that even if someone nicked it, it was possible to identify it in some future pile and pinch it back.

The traditional enmity between Trinity and Balliol had not been mollified by our co-operation on the river because "Mr Bolton then rose to excite the public by his oratory to do something ourselves about the offensive song sung by a neighbouring college. Then at the end of a stirring speech he suggested that Mr Landon's ping-pong days were over and that in future a member of the JCR should see to the buying of ping-pong bats". Apart from this ramble off the point, the complaint about the singing of the infamous Gordouli –"If I were a bloody Trinity man, I would, I would —" followed by suggestions of what he should do –by the people over the wall was taken further by an entry in the suggestions book signed by Duncan Davies and N.J. Hopkinson asking that Balliol men billeted in Trinity have a table to themselves.

The fact that there was a war on clearly led to Jimmy Somner noting that "Mr Holladay, in uniform, then rose to wonder whether he had any right to say anything; then just to be on the safe side he said nothing and sat down" but the determined Mr Bolton entered the fray again, supported by David Van Zwannenberg, to suggest that the President's ducks should be muzzled at all times and especially in the early morning. Their exposure to the quacking of the President's ducks is explained by them being on Staircase 9 which overlooks the President's garden. It was suggested that impersonal remarks when at tea with the President might work wonders. What a pleasant Edwardian atmosphere this paints of Mr Weaver holding civilised discourse with his undergraduates over cups of tea. No doubt in Summer this could have been in the President's garden surrounded by groups of the offending ducks.

The domestic concerns of the college can be found most clearly by the items that occur in the suggestions book. For example, Derek Dawson, having taken up residence on Staircase 11 complained that the windows needed cleaning. Ray Peters reflected on the shortage of matches that was to irritate everyone increasingly as the war progressed. Roger Hammick sensibly suggested that the walls under arches and staircase entrances be painted white to help in the black-out.

David Aiers and Bill Pakenham-Walsh both righteously complained at the lights being left on in the JCR when no-one was using it and Nigel Mathew asked for two sets of mustard, salt and pepper to be provided on each table. He also asked for gummed labels to be provided to enable envelopes to be re-used. Wartime shortages were beginning to tell. This was particularly so in the case of food rationing, and there were some pretty disgusting substitutes for some of the pre-war staples of the breakfast table. Tinned bacon from America and sausages called Soya Links, which had to be unrolled from grease-proof paper after being slid out of the tin, took the place of gammon slices and juicy pork in skins. We could still get ham of a sort and a plate of ham and potatoes at lunch time cost 1/9. A plaintive request from Ivor Lewisohn for the reinstatement of sandwiches and an equally heart-felt plea from Shoeten-Sack for hot pudding at dinner received a lengthy reply from the food committee.

"The question of sandwiches need not be raised any more. It is a matter of supply and staff. We are eating into reserves of tinned meat as it is and sandwiches are too extravagant a way of using it up. There is also the butter question which would not even be remedied if a sandwich eater gave up his butter ration. It seems that sandwiches are out for the duration. However there will be hot pudding at night twice a week in future and in order to make up for the dubious `lease-lend bacon' there will be fried potatoes as breakfast twice a week. But here again the question of staff makes it difficult."

It is interesting to note that the college had a private supply of tinned meat quietly hoarded away for which we had to thank Philip Landon's foresight. The fact that such hoarding was officially frowned on and technically illegal would not have worried some-one whose advice even learned judges paraded to his rooms in the Garden Quad to seek.

There were some quite heated exchanges, mostly centring on the lavatories and bathrooms.

"Sir, what has happened to the curtains in the bath house so that British privacy may be once more obtained when bathing?" enquired M.E. Lock. "Yes, why have they disappeared? I can think of a reason but it doesn't seem quite nice to put it here," added the redoubtable Simon Partridge. Jimmy Somner's reply was brusque.

"They have disappeared because they were rotting - if they can be replaced they shall be."

John Boxshall and N. Anderson requested "bumph in the JCR rears" and Peter Currie not only complained of the shortage but also criticised the quality. He was told that there was a large supply of wartime quality but he roused the ire of Master of the Rolls Roger Hammick who castigated him with the phrase that became one of the most repeated cliches of the war, "Don't you know there's a war on?"

The lavatory paper wrangle surfaced again in another form when D.G.B. Jones, obviously failing to discern the extreme conservatism of the Trinity undergraduate, questioned why the Daily Herald was not available in the JCR. Peter Currie replied, "I suggest that it would be a good thing if Mr Jones discovers if he has any supporters in his claim for a paper of rather doubtful value." This was countersigned by David Van Zwannenberg, Simon Partridge, N. Anderson, P. Flint, J.B.P. Quinlan, T.G.A. Kingan, M.E. Lock, R.R. Thompson, W. Pakenham-Walsh and J. Butler, which should have put paid to the Labour-supporting Daily Herald but David Van Zwannenberg subsequently produced this wrathful entry, "As the JCR decisively vetoed the buying of the Daily Herald, may I ask why this foul excrescence of a paper is in the JCR this morning? Might I suggest that it should be used in solving the difficulties of the Master of the Rolls."

Derek Dawson asked if there could be better black-out in the rears so that there could be more light, a plea supported by all of us who were compulsive readers. He received a crushing anonymous reply, "Why do you want to throw light on the subject? Do it in the dark!" If it appears from these few extracts that Colonel Blimp might have felt at home among us it would probably not be far off the mark. And, of course, Colonel Blimp was the creation of the cartoonist Low in the despised Daily Herald.

Our reading matter followed the conventional lines of

almost every Gentlemen's Club or Officer's Mess. Most of the papers had shrunk to eight or twelve pages to save news print but there was still a remarkable variety available. The Times and the Daily Telegraph led the more serious broadsheets followed by the Daily Mail, the Daily Express and the News Chronicle. The Daily Sketch and the Daily Mirror were the only two tabloids. On Sunday we took the Sunday Times and the Observer. Columnists played a big part in attracting our readership, Peter Simple in the Telegraph, Collie Knox in the Mail, William Hickey in the Express which also had the inimitable Beachcomber, and the acerbic Cassandra in the Mirror. On Sunday, James Agate and Dilys Powell wrote the theatre and film reviews in the Sunday Times, competing with Ivor Brown and Carol Lejeune in the Observer. The Daily Express had the additional attraction of the Giles cartoons and the Daily Mirror provided the daily ration of titillation with a strip cartoon character called Jane, who did just that at least once a week. Those of us clinging to our childhood could follow the adventures of Teddy Tail or Pip, Squeak and Wilfrid in the Sketch.

Our magazine reading encompassed the Illustrated London News, Punch, the Sporting and Dramatic, the Tatler and Picture Post.

There were also some excellent literary magazines such as the Strand, Blackwood's and Argosy and the racier but no less intelligent Men Only. Every term this array would come under the earnest scrutiny of the assembled JCR to decide what we would regard as suitable reading for the ensuing term. It is perhaps, a commentary on one's state of mind at the time that it is only the lighter writers that I can remember. Who the leading war correspondents or serious commentators were I have no recollection.

The Jazz Jamboree and Margaret's involvement with dance bands and musicians in her new job with the ENSA broadcasting division gave me a new interest in the professional music world and provided a good point of contact when I became involved in the formation of the Oxford University Rhythm Club.

The prime mover in this was a chap in University College called Derek Dowdall. As the son of a GP in Hebden Bridge he seemed to have spent an inordinate amount of time in the night clubs and dives of London acquiring an encyclopaedic knowledge of British jazz and jazz men. I suppose that we must have met in the confines of the listening booths in the basement of Taphouses where we used to crowd to hear the latest records. Swing was the pop music of the day and, in common with most young people of my day (I don't think that "teenagers" had been invented then), I collected the latest offerings of Artie Shaw, Benny Goodman, Harry James, Gene Krupa, and Bob Crosby. Bob Crosby's drummer, Ray Bauduc, was my particular favourite and I had bought a drumming primer at Acott's called "150 Progressive Drum Rhythms" which he was supposed to have written. Nevil Macready had rather more esoteric tastes preferring Jimmy Lunceford, Duke Ellington and Count Basie. We all enjoyed Fats Waller for his exuberance and fun but he hadn't at that time reached the cult status he achieved after his death. But it was Derek who introduced us to Josh White, Bunk Johnson, Sydney Bechet, Tommy Ladnier and, indeed, Louis Armstrong.

One day we were gathered in Elliston's when Derek came in with a copy of the "Melody Maker", which reported on the activities of a series of Rhythm Clubs created throughout Britain to encourage the playing and greater understanding of jazz. Two journalists, Bill Elliot and Sinclair Traill were assigned to the task and would be available to visit any group of people wishing to form a club. We thought that it seemed to be a good idea and instantly formed ourselves into an ad hoc committee to bring it about. We instantly elected Derek to be President, Secretary, and anything else that required actual work and dispersed to await developments. The Melody Maker people were delighted to receive an invitation from Oxford and agreed to send their men to inaugurate our club as soon as we could get it officially recognised. Derek managed to persuade a rather dazed don, Professor Levens of Merton, to be the Senior member required to register the club with the authorities. Notices were painstakingly typed out and posted

At the first meeting of the Oxford University Rhythm Club Sinclair Traill is on the extreme left (front row), and Derek Dowdall, president, is standing (with scarf round his neck) between Mr. and Mrs. Bill Elliott.

FIRST UNIVERSITY RHYTHM CLUB INAUGURATED

THE English Universities have always shown a great interest in jazz, and it is with great pleasure that we publish details of the first University Rhythm Club.

Oxford has the distinction, and the opening meeting was held in the Taylorian on Wednesday, October 29, to an enthusiastic audience of 250 undergraduates.

Bill Elliott and Sinclair Traill travelled from London and Leamington, respectively, to give the opening recitals, and a great reception was accorded them.

Present plans are for a weekly meeting, and the club officials are: Derek Dowdall (University College), president; John Young (Merton College), Brian Parker (B. and C. College), joint secretaries; Maurice Hodgson (Merton College), treasurer.

Accounts of future meetings will be published in the "M.M." Rhythm Club news weekly.

hopefully on college notice boards announcing our inaugural meeting in the Taylorian. Our meeting was going to be inhibited by the fact that none of us had any form of record player other than our standard wind-up portables, which made a lecture on jazz, or any other kind of music, difficult in a large and echoing lecture theatre. Amazingly about two hundred people turned up to be told that we were the first University in Britain to have formed such a club. Well done us! The Melody Maker ran a story to this effect in their issue of November 8th, giving us our club number 14 and printing a rather smudgy photo of Bill Elliott with his wife and Sinclair Traill with Derek and me and the rest of the committee leering over their shoulders. Just for the record, the committee was listed as Derek (President), John Young of Merton and Brian Parker, BNC, (joint secretaries) and Maurice Hodgson of Merton as treasurer. It was a good start but obviously we had to offer something better than gramophone records played on a portable wind-up gramophone if we were to keep our membership let alone persuade others to join us.

Derek suggested that we should invite guest musicians or even whole bands to come to Oxford to play for us. In 1941 London was still having some very unpleasant raids, so we gambled on the hope that the players might be only too glad to get out into the country for an afternoon. Obviously the only day most of them would be available would be Sunday. With the brashness of youth we decided that no fees would be offered but that we would pay all fares and wine and dine our guests as liberally as possible. Strangely the only opposition we had came from the Bandits who decided that the Rhythm Club was a rival organisation and that if anyone wanted a jazz club they should run it. The lure of acting as a backing band for some top musicians failed to move them. Undaunted, we pressed on and hired a hall in George Street and put out posters announcing our first open meeting. Join the club by paying five shillings at the door.

We had managed to get the ideal band to start things off, Johnny Claes and his Claepigeons who we had seen at the Palladium a few weeks earlier. Johnny was a Belgian millionaire playboy who enjoyed motor racing and Dixieland jazz. He had escaped from the Germans with his precious trumpet and formed a band in London with some of the best players in the country. Not all of them could come to Oxford but a swinging quintet arrived including Derek Neville (saxophone), Norman Stenfalt (piano), Peter Needham (bass), and a young drummer making his professional debut called Bobby Midgeley. Our only worry came when about three hundred people came to hear them. It created an ideal atmosphere, an over-crowded, smoke-filled room with a first class showman. We started decorously with a serious discussion on jazz in general led by Jimmy Sylvester, one of our committee members, and illustrated with gramophone records. Then Johnny Claes and his boys took over. They played all the popular standards of the day; "Honeysuckle Rose", "Deep Purple", "Rose Room", a long twelve-bar blues and a driving version of "Doggin' Around" which really got the room jumping and, in time, became almost the Club signature tune.

Afterwards we went back to my room in Trinity and listened to some new recordings the band had just made. Altogether it was great success and from that moment the O.U. Rhythm Club never looked back.

The following Sunday found us in London in a crowd of over a thousand crushed in to the HMV No.1 Studio in Abbey Road for the Melody Maker Jam Session. This had been set up on the lines of the American Downbeat magazine session with invited artists chosen by a readership poll. In this case there were twenty-four performers who were formed into four groups led in turn by clarinetists Harry Parry, Carl Barriteau, and Frank Weir, with saxophonist Buddy Featherstonehaugh taking the fourth group. The audience was almost as interesting as the players including Geraldo, Victor Sylvester, Max Bacon, David Miller, Christopher Stone, Eric Winstone, and George Elrick, all of whom were star names in 1941. George Shearing was spotted in the audience and persuaded to join the players and David Miller took over from the corps of comperes, Wally Moody, Edgar Jackson, Bill Elliott and Ray

Sonin, to introduce a contingent of survivors from the Ken Johnson Band. It was the first time that British musicians had been recorded in this way and, while they were well known for their ability to sight-read the most complicated arrangements, their improvisational skills had never really been tested at this level. In fact the final results, reduced to a series of 10-inch 78s, were only fair but it was an exciting experience which made our Rhythm Club membership seem worthwhile.

We formed a scratch band back in Oxford to accompany visiting soloists and later in the term the young, up and coming George Shearing came to defeat us with a boogie waltz long before anyone had thought of "Take Five" with me on drums, Jimmy Sylvester on bass and Bert Shaw on guitar. Then the Bandits joined in and Frank Dixon led a fine jam session with Mervyn Brown on tenor sax, Eric Derge trumpet, Dennis or was it Derek Cawston on piano with Jimmy Sylvester, Bert Shaw and Alan Lazarus on drums.

Cawston, Sylvester, Shaw and I hired a studio and made an acetate recording of "Tuxedo Junction" which we sold to the members. Mervyn slightly spoiled the effect by failing to get his sax exactly in tune with the piano. In subsequent meetings we entertained and were entertained by Cyril Blake, Dick Katz, Reg Owen, Art Thompson, Danny Deans and George Fierstone who put his stick through my Leedy snare-drum but taught me a lot about how to play the hi-hat. There was also a musician we only knew as "The Dreamer". He arrived wobbly drunk and was propped up in a chair where he played the clarinet like an angel all afternoon before disappearing as mysteriously as he had come. We thought he might have come from Henry Hall's band but never found out for sure. It was that kind of a club. In the end we had over a thousand paid up members which Derek gleefully discovered was more than the Conservatives.

We never entirely shook off the feeling of suspicion that always seems to attach itself to the jazz world. After the George Shearing session, which took place in the Univ JCR, we repaired to Derek's room for drinks and general chatter. I suppose we were making a certain amount of noise and, because there were about a dozen of us, we were sprawled around the room, sitting on the floor, on the bed and wherever a space could be found. There were several girls in the party. In due course the Dean was summoned by the college porter to break up what had been described to him as "an erotic party." The Dean was Harold Wilson, who hadn't at that time decided to adopt the strong North Country accent which his choice of career later demanded.

"Mr Dowdall, may I see you outside for a moment?"

Derek unwound himself from the girls on the bed and followed the Dean out into the corridor. A few moments later he returned looking theatrically chastened and told us we had all better get out. We trouped down the stairs into the quad, past the Shelley statue which still bore the faint scars of the attentions which had led to the rustication of one of Univ's wilder men for "painting on his pubic hair and painting his balls red."

The Sunday afternoon sessions of the Rhythm Club became a regular feature of our lives. It survived the war and, when several of us returned from the forces, became extremely active. Yet strangely, in spite of its popularity, no trace of its existence could be found in the University archives.

As a shadow for the future, while I was checking the back copies of the Melody Maker in the British Newspaper Library for some of these dates and times, I found a letter to the editor extolling the virtues of a film called "Beat Me Daddy Eight To The Bar" featuring Wingy Mannone and his band. "Everyone should make a point of seeing it" said the writer who must have been fourteen or fifteen at the time. It may well have been his first printed critique. It was signed Kenneth P. Tynan, Edgbaston.

Outside the College there was a lot to be done. There were the Rhythm Club meetings to be organised and, armed with my newly acquired theatrical skills, I started to collect an inventory of all the theatrical equipment held by the Colleges to be pooled within the projected O.U. Theatre Guild. Every college had a stock of lights, scenery and even costumes which they seldom used more than once a year. By pooling them we could save a good deal of money by not having to hire lights from Strand Electric or costumes from Nathans or Bermans or Foxes. Everyone co-operated on the reasonable proviso that they would have first use of their own equipment. This would hardly be a problem because it was unlikely that two Colleges would deliberately clash production dates. It had the major advantage that we could rig the Taylorian early in the term and leave much of the lighting and flats there.

Nevill Coghill and Glynne Wickham were deep into their plans for the forthcoming production of "Hamlet". Our tutorials tended to become production conferences and Nevill's floor was covered in designs and stage plans. Nevill's production was sufficiently innovative for it to have been felt necessary for him to explain, in a programme note, what would have been standard practice in Shakespeare's day and has since become so in the modern theatre.

"We have abandoned scenery", he wrote, "as a post not to be defended and hope you will accept the convention that no room has a stick of furniture except what happens to be immediately necessary for some player to use in a particular scene. Furnishings must be functional. The use of an apron stage is partly dictated by the nature of the play ... (soliloquies cannot gain their full force unless they are treated as intimate confessions to an almost priestlike audience: even Claudius will use you so) ...and partly by the smallness of the permanent stage. The smallness of the apron is due to the fact that players on it could not be seen from the balcony if it were larger."

The set was entirely of black curtains with a small rostrum up stage. The original intention to build a thrust stage of Elizabethan proportions had to be abandoned because, as Nevill points out, the actors couldn't then be seen from the balcony, so we had to settle for only about five feet being added to the front of the tiny stage. To try to make this area seem larger, I had devised a lighting plot of truly Hulbertian dimensions involving pools of light moving about the stage so that the whole set was never fully lit and lighting was angled off the back cloth to increase the impression of a depth of blackness. To do this involved the use of no less than twenty two one thousand or five hundred watt spots. The electrician who had to rig this and link it to the switch board was Nickie Pomfret who ensured that the fuses didn't blow by the judicious use of meccano in the fuse box, and had to sit nightly at a bank of dimmers glowing red hot in the dim light at the top of the prompt side stairs. How we didn't burn the place down is now a mystery but I believe that we melted sufficient of the insulation off the wiring to make it necessary to rewire the building some time later, but it may not have been all our fault as others also used the building.

I established my prompt corner behind the curtain near the switch board on a small table surrounded by a radiogram, a bass drum, my snare drum, a tubular bell, a small thunder sheet and a wind machine. In the days before tape recorders everything had to be done by hand. The music had been chosen by Lord Berners and the opening was to Cesar Franck's D Minor Symphony. This was on a 12-inch record (78 r.p.m. of course) with a cue marked in chinagraph to start the chimes at midnight. There wasn't room for an assistant so that I had to cue the lights, hit my tubular bell, fade the music and get the tabs open to reveal the sentry hopefully standing in the light of a single spot while the opening actors came down the centre aisle. It was an exciting performance for the stage management not least for the logistics of getting the players on and off the stage from the dungeon down below which housed the dressing rooms. Philip Trower, David Warwick and Byng Husband acted as ASMs when they weren't being Rosencrantz and Guildernstern, Messenger, Priest or Courtiers.

A further complication revealed itself when Nevill decided to play the Ghost of King Hamlet himself. Having been so deeply absorbed in producing the show he hadn't really learnt his lines so I had to position myself in the wing nearest to his point of appearance to prompt him. It took a bit of time to guage the appropriate level of voice I could use without making it appear that we were working a puppet show

The stage of the Taylor Institute hasn't changed (1994). My prompt corner was to the right of the doors. Through the doors was the switchboard where the dimmers glowed red. The curtain on the left marks the back of the stage!

but at least by the time of the performance before an audience I had stopped Nevill answering my prompts with an audible "What?"

Our only disastrous performance was the Saturday matinee when Glynne lost Hamlet's personal prop recorder and went on with a comb and paper which made him appear decidedly mad, and the clock which I had borrowed for the prompt corner suddenly revealed itself to be an alarm which came in smartly on the cue "To sleep perchance to dream." Altogether we gave a good account of ourselves. Glynne's Hamlet was a cautious introspective reading of the part and Robert Harris was very complimentary when he came round after the final performance. Robert Helpman paid Nevill a sincere compliment by using his finale, with Hamlet being carried off upstage while a single spot irised out on his ashen face, as the opening of his Hamlet ballet.

Two things that stand out now when looking at the programme are the remarkable shortness of the interval, a mere eight minutes, and the fact that, not being allowed to charge, we thought that a florin, two shillings or twenty pence, a reasonable amount to ask for a donation. Jack Becke, immaculate in evening dress, organised this and added a little tone to the front of house. But, for me, the most interesting thing about the programme is Nevill Coghill's notes about his production because they reflect so accurately the voice and presence of the man and his truly amazing diffidence.

It was a pity that our opening coincided with the arrival in Oxford of Ivor Novello's "The Dancing Years" which may explain the comparative lack of notice we received from the local press but John Bryson, a Balliol Don, wrote a rather waggish review with comments like "this Hamlet must have still been in his first term when he was recalled from Wittenberg; he can't have gone very deep in philosophy but he had certainly joined the W.U.D.S. for he had an excellent memory and had already learned to attack a soliloquoy naturally and to act with confidence and some conviction." So much for Glynne Wickham's youthful appearance. But Bryson hadn't finished with his fun. "With such younglings (sic!) as men of the world, we must of necessity have an Ophelia who looked more like retiring to a nursery than a nunnery." He pointed out that it must have been nice for Hamlet to have as a friend "Horatio, quite twice his years." On the technical side he had my sympathy. "Once again the Taylorian stage was the villain of the piece (when, oh when, shall we have a University theatre?)" He thought that the apron was a great success in bringing the actors into closer and easier touch with the audience in the soliloquoys. His only real niggle was aimed at my faithful henchmen when "the Court of five, nicely graded by height, lined up on a platform above the grave and stayed there looking for all the world as if they were getting ready to

Glynne Wickham's design for the cover of the Hamlet programme

By kind permission of the Vice-Chancellor and the Mayor of Oxford.
FRIENDS OF THE O.U.D.S. PRESENT

HAMLET

By William Shakespeare.
Characters in order of their appearance:

Fransisco .... GEORGE ALLEN	First Player .... CHRISTOPHER PALLIS
Bernardo .... HENRY TALBOT-HARVEY	Second Player .... JOHN ELEY
Marcellus .... JAMES LANDON	Third Player .... ROGER LANCELYN GREEN
Horatio .... HALLAM FORDHAM	Fortinbras .... BENNY TOTTENHAM
The Ghost of King Hamlet .... NEVILL COGHILL	A Captain .... JOHN ELEY
King Claudius .... QUENTIN DOBSON	Messenger .... BYNG HUSBAND
Gertrude .... SONIA SOUTH	First Grave-Digger ... ROGER LANCELYN GREEN
Polonius .... BRYAN HENSHAW	Second Grave Digger .... ESMOND SMITH
Laertes .... JOHN GOLDINGHAM	Priest .... HENRY TALBOT-HARVEY
Hamlet .... GLYNNE WICKHAM	Osric .... ROGNWALD GUNN
Ophelia .... MARGARET BOWDEN	Ladies of the Court .. MARY HALL, ALISON MARK
Rosencrantz .... PHILIP TROWER	Courtiers .... ROGER GREEN, BYNG HUSBAND
Guildenstern .... DAVID WARWICK	(On Saturday Bernado and the Priest will be played by BYNG HUSBAND)

The Play produced by Nevill Coghill
The Action takes place in and about the Palace of Elsinore, Denmark.
There will be ONE INTERVAL OF EIGHT MINUTES during which A FLORIN COLLECTION WILL BE TAKEN.

The Music chosen by Lord Berners.
The Costumes by Nathan & Co. from designs by Diana Yeldham-Taylor.
The Lighting by Nickie Pomfret.
Stage Manager: John Harper-Nelson.
Business and Front of the House Manager: Jack Becke.
The Programme Cover designed by Glynne Wickham.
The duel arranged by Anthony Hill.

WHO ARE THE FRIENDS OF THE O.U.D.S.?

You are; and so is anyone who helps in any way to diminish the heavy debts from which the O.U.D.S. was struggling to free itself just before the war. The debt is still, unfortunately, large. So please be generous. We are not allowed to charge for tickets; but who would take advantage of that?

PRACTICAL NOTE.

This play, uncut would take rather more than four hours. We hope to play it in under three hours; spectators will therefore not be surprised to find it heavily cut; I apologise to all those who are disappointed at finding their favourite speeches left out. . . some there will certainly be. . . . I have cut on the principle that all necessary information as to action must be retained; because one MUST be clear what the story is. I do not feel I have been quite successful even in this; especially at the points where Hamlet is sent to England after his killing of polonius and where the King is arranging the treachorous duel that Laertes is to fight with Hamlet. I have also done my utmost to retain all the most celebrated passages in this celebrated play; but as almost every line, and certainly every scene contains a "quotation", I must have failed.

We have abandoned scenery as a post not to be defended and hope you will accept the convention thay no room has a stick of furniture except what happens to be immediately necessary for some player to use in that particular scene. Furnishings must be functional. The use of an Apron stage is partly dictated by the nature of the play . . . (soliloquies cannot gain their full force unless they are treated as intimate confessions to an almost priestlike audience; even Claudius will use you so) . . . and partly by the smallness of the permanent stage. The smallness of the Apron is de to the fact that players on it could not be seen from the Balcony as if it were larger.

THE "GUSH SIDE".

Why does Hamlet delay? Is he Mad? Pretending? Are people sane who pretend to be mad? Too intellectual? Thinking too precisely on the event? Cowardice? Melancholia? Oedipus complex? No delay, no play? A mere enigma? Emotion in excess of the facts? Can emotion be in excess of these facts?—a Mother's incestuous adultery, a Father's murder by an Uncle, a Sweetheart's betrayal? Why is the Closet scene more important than the Play-within-the-play? Is that why the King is not killed at his prayers? Should Rosencrantz be distinguishable from Guildenstern? Why is Yorick the Jester dead? Is it credible that a man could jump into his sister's grave? And fight in his Sweetheart's? Does is matter whether it is credible or not? . . .

Speculation could go on for ever . . . .
      MAR.   But do not go on with it.
      HOR.   No, by no means . . .
                What if it tempt you toward the flood my Lord,
                Or to the dreadful summit of the cliff
                That beetles o'er his base into the sea,
                And there assume some other horrible form
                Which might deprive your sovereignty of reason,
                And draw you into madness? Think of it!

* * * * * * *

The prosperity of a Play lies in the ears of those that hear it.

N.C.

PERFORMANCES

Reserved seats bookable at Messrs. Acotts, High Street, Oxford.
WEDNESDAY, NOVEMBER 26 at 7.30p.m.   FRIDAY, NOVEMBER 28 at 7.30p.m.
THURSDAY, NOVEMBER 27 at 7.30p.m.   SATURDAY, NOVEMBER 29 at 7.30p.m.
                    SATURDAY (Matinee) at 2.15 p.m.
in
THE TAYLOR INSTITUTION
1941

burst into the quintet from the Meistersingers." The grave scene in Hamlet is notoriously difficult and obviously we hadn't solved it. Still he remarked that "the gramophone records - specially chosen by Lord Berners - were a feature. They ranged from Bach to Cesar Franck." And he could have added that they were a nightmare to keep in order and cue on time.

If you detect some Donnish waspishness in Bryson's review you may be right. Nevill once said to me, "If you read what Bryson has to say and disagree with it you won't go far wrong."

Still we made a profit as Nevill's calculations showed:-

By collection	£27-	11-	3	Stage Manager (Sundries)	£4-	2-	10
Sale of programmes	£43-	5-	0	Hessian 25 yards	£2-	5-	6
	£58-	6-	11	Journey to London	£1-	9-	0
	£129-	3-	2	Head Porter Gratuity	£3-	0-	0
Less expenses	£83-	17-	1	Taylor Institute 5 performances	£20-	0-	0
	£45-	6-	1	Hire of lorry	£1-	0-	0
				Printer	£16-	7-	6
				Nathan Wigs	£15-	0-	0
				Lighting. Lowe & Oliver	£4-	15-	0
				Curtains	£3-	0-	0
				Diana Yeldham-Taylor,Designer	£3-	3-	0
				Nathans, carriage etc	£4-	0-	0
				Hill Upton, lighting	£3-	8-	0
				Lowe & Oliver (breakages)	£2-	11-	3
					£83-	17-	1

£45-6-1 went into the Friends of the OUDS coffers, and if we hadn't have dropped a spot it would have been a bit more.

As a side line, one of my stage crew, who later took over as the Friends of the OUDS Stage Manager, had to be led back to Magdalen after dark because, as a scientist, he was taking part in an experiment in Vitamin D deficiency. There was a theory that a lot of Vitamin D improved night vision and he was testing the corollary that a deficiency caused night blindness. The night fighter ace Cats-Eyes Cunningham attributed his excellent night vision to an increased intake of Vitamin D, which did great things for the sale of carrots but was, in fact, part of an elaborate deception to keep from the Germans the knowledge that we had developed air-borne radar. Whether my friend was

Glynne Wickham as Hamlet

knowingly involved in this deception I don't know but I don't think that he was pretending to be blind in the dark. Unfortunately his name isn't on the programme so his sacrifice must go unsung. But we should have been aware of the existence of radar, or at least of some advanced electronic gadgetry, because a large number of us were recruited to become labourers on a building project laying the foundations for a series of huge wireless aerials somewhere in the hills. Each morning for about two weeks a row of busses lined up in the Broad to take a raggle taggle assortment of young men to an unknown location where we dug trenches and filled them up with concrete which we mixed by hand on huge wooden platforms. The regular navvies were amused that we wore gloves to avoid blisters but were amazed at the speed we worked. The local press called us the "kid glove navvies" and we were impressed at the amount of pay we got.

I think it was more per hour than I had got per performance in the theatre and certainly more than I later got as a Second Lieutenant.

Our Shakespearean effort was not the only major production in the Taylorian. The Experimental Theatre Club had mounted Pirandello's "Henry IV" the week before using our pooled equipment. This was produced by Michael Flanders who also played the lead. The Oxford Magazine described him as "an actor exceptionally gifted in portraying intensity of thought and feeling." His co-producer was John Cunningham-Craig and the cast included Roy Porter, Rosemary Brown, Michael Palliser, David Davison and Simon Frazer.

There was still a bit of activity on the river. Someone had decided that because the four and a half mile course on the Tideway was no longer available, we should inaugurate a long distance race on the Isis. A good stretch of river was found down stream of Iffley Lock, past Radley to the railway bridge. There wasn't enough room for side-by-side racing so we practised for a time trial as in the London Head of the River. Our combined Trinity/Balliol crew had every chance of winning as we seemed to be better over the longer distance and our practice times were certainly impressive. There was one section of the course where

Cynthia in her costume for "Full Swing"

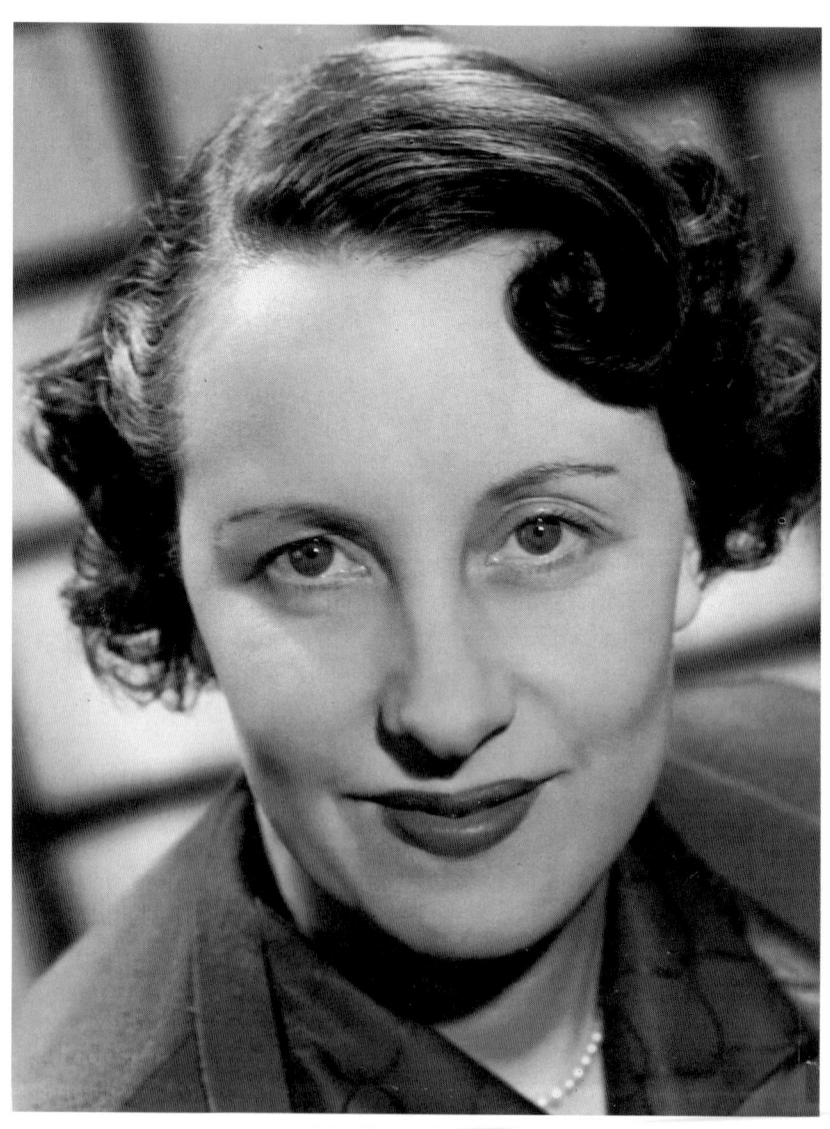

My Sister Margaret

there was a sharp bend round an island which could only be negotiated at racing speed by the stroke side oars paddling light while the bow side oars put in three or four special strong ones. We were rather pleased with this ploy as the others had resorted to relying on the cox putting on such heavy rudder that the boat was slowed right down. So we approached the start full of confidence and set off in the sure knowledge that we had mastered the technique of fast cornering. That was when our number three broke his oar. Not a fatal crack but enough to make it impossible for him to give it his full weight. Even then I think we came second and were not disgraced. These long rows were happy affairs and we ended our collaboration on a high note. It proved that Trinity and Balliol can occasionally pull together.

As Christmas approached the world began to change for all of us. The Germans were bogged down in Russia and the Japanese attack on Pearl Harbour had forced the Americans into the war. There was a general feeling that, no matter what setbacks there were in the future, the tide was about to turn and we would inevitably come out victorious. There was even apprehension that the war might be over before we had taken part in it. In London there were significant signs that confidence was returning. New shows were coming into the West End and restaurants and night clubs were booming in spite of rationing and shortages. Margaret, Nevil Macready and I went out to Harrow-on-the-Hill for the final night of the Hulbert Follies. There was an end of term feeling about it as people who had toured together for a year said their farewells. But there was optimism because Jack Hulbert's new show "Full Swing" was already in rehearsal and was scheduled to open at the Palace in February. "Up and Doing" which had dealt us such a blow in Manchester was now at the Saville Theatre. There were still occasional air raids but we had returned to our old haunts round Cambridge Circus and Soho.

Margaret had settled into her new career with ENSA. Her office was in one of the dressing rooms of the little Fortune Theatre across the road from the Theatre Royal and a pub opposite the main Drury Lane portico called the Falstaff became our principal meeting place. It was while heading for the Falstaff one day that I noticed that there was a poster outside the theatre proclaiming "Come the four corners of the world and we shall shock them". In view of the reputation of some of the ENSA concert parties, there was a supercilious sneer that ENSA stood for Every Night Something Awful, I told Margaret that I thought this slogan was rather inappropriate. It was removed shortly after.

Nevil's family had moved from their temporary quarters in the Park Lane Hotel to a flat in 55, Park Lane which gave us a good base from which to sally forth to such illicit joys as the bottle party night clubs like the Nuthouse. or Cabaret or the Suivi where Harry Gold and his Pieces of Eight was the resident band. There were also two afternoon clubs called the Gay Nineties and The Vanity Fair which we found useful to meet friends in. One of these was a rather wild man called Tim Jenkins who inveigled us into a bet that you could drink the clock round in London without breaking the law. We found that this was possible by going to the pubs round the markets from Smithfield to Billingsgate to Covent Garden by which time the daytime opening hours had started but we were defeated by the closure of all pubs from three to five in the afternoon. So we lost our bet and resorted once more to the private places. Tim, at the time, was pursuing Celia the daughter of band leader Syd Lipton and it was while we were in the Suivi that he and Celia disappeared for about half an hour from the party. It was not the sort of place you could have a private smooch and Tim had solved the problem by hiring a taxi and getting it to drive round Hyde Park. Celia's mother was with us and expressed her disapproval in no uncertain terms on their return. But it was a ruse to remember.

Len Hunt had moved to Hatchetts in Piccadilly where the band included such names as Stephane Grapelly, George Shearing, Carl Barriteau, Leslie 'Jiver' Hutchinson, the Deniz Brothers and Tommy Bromley, still on crutches. This became our favourite haunt and was enhanced by being in the basement under the Berkeley Hotel which made the restaurant virtually an air raid shelter. When things were fairly quiet, Len would let me sit in on the drums. He also played in a band led by Jack Leon for ENSA broadcasts and recordings which was part of the National Service required of musicians who had obtained deferments. One of Margaret's first jobs was timing and assisting the production of this group. The boys in the band seemed to indulge in endless dealings in such commodities as clothing coupons and other black market scarcities that Margaret used to refer to them as the Thieves Kitchen. As assistant to Stephen Williams, a producer of great experience who had come from the commercial station Radio Luxemburg, Margaret helped to produce such shows as "Break for Music", "London Carries On" and the "ENSA Half Hour." These broadcasts were mostly done from the stage of the Fortune Theatre or the stalls bar of Drury Lane which had been converted into a studio. "Break for Music" involved taking a leading band and supporting artists to a factory canteen to record a live performance. By the time I arrived for the Christmas vacation, she was firmly established as a studio secretary, timing programmes, checking scripts and continuity. The radio programmes were recorded on disc and then dubbed onto 12-inch 78s for distribution to forces broadcasting stations overseas.

Wartime regulations made sure that every word was scripted and the scripts rigidly adhered to. This used to cause some bother to comedians who were used to ad libbing but was enforced to make sure that no spy could pass secret messages over the air waves. Also secret messages were passed through BBC broadcasts to the resistance fighters in Europe and they couldn't take the risk that a wrong code word was inadvertantly put over. In these sometimes subtle ways the war impinged on every aspect of our lives.

The head of ENSA publicity was W. MacQueen Pope. He was the PR man for Drury Lane Theatre before the war and the leading historian of the theatre and so never moved out of his office when he changed jobs. He delighted in showing people round his beloved theatre with its huge stage, paint shops and set construction workshops. For those who go to Drury Lane the size of the stage can be judged from the fact that the proscenium arch is exactly half way up the building so that there is as much space behind as the whole auditorium. Now this huge area was working flat out constructing fit-up sets for the stream of concert parties that were being sent all over the world where-ever there were troops to be entertained. He showed me the famous Green Room where murder had been committed, the damaged Dress Circle where a bomb had landed but mercifully failed to explode properly, and the Promenade where the ghost was supposed to walk. Down on the stage a standard portable stage had been erected where each show was given its final rehearsal before being sent off. Singers, dancers, comedians, ventriloquists, conjurors, acrobats and actors all passed through the ENSA machine before repairing to the Falstaff for refreshment. Here it was interesting to meet old time stars of the Music Halls like Bunny Doyle -"You don't know what a tough audience is until you've played Barnsley"- and glamourous stars like Florence Desmond and Evelyn Laye who all entertained the troops for the standard fee of £10 a week. Later Cynthia was to join them and become one of the most sought after soubrettes.

For Nevil it was a special pleasure to follow the footsteps of his famous forebear the Great Macready who was reported to have stormed into the wings during a performance, dragged the prompter onto the stage and flattened him with a blow, before explaining to the audience "The villain prompted me in me Grand Pause." Thank goodness nothing like that occurred in "Hamlet".

The parent body of ENSA was the Navy, Army, and Air Force Institute –the NAAFI– which ran all the Garrison Theatres and Cinemas. It too had its detractors who called it No Aim Ambition or Flaming Interest. In order to publicise ENSA and to raise funds for the various Forces Benevolent Funds, all–star concerts were sometimes organised. This mingling of star artists often led to tensions especially where the billing was concerned as ENSA insisted that this should always be in strict alphabetical order. The only star who refused to perform when he saw that his name wasn't at the top was George Formby although one or two others had to be threatened with a call to the newspapers to make them concur. Nevertheless I saw the sort of situation that could arise when I went with Margaret to a big hospital in Woolwich for the recording of the ENSA Christmas Special. Geraldo's Orchestra was there with all it's star vocalists, Dorothy Carless, Doreen Villiers, Len Camber, Jackie Hunter, plus a crowd of others including a young Pat Kirkwood. At the run-through, the show over-ran considerably so cuts had to be made. It was Margaret's unenviable job to tell the artists the producer's decision.

Pat Kirkwood's husband, who was her agent, charged up shouting "My Pat 'asn't come all this way to do just two numbers." When he threatened to withdraw her from the show I suddenly heard Margaret shout, "Shut up! If you don't like it, take your tatty little piece home!" Basil Dean and all the ENSA top brass were there and so far from getting Margaret the sack it was the making of her. Basil Dean, who was a notorious martinet in the theatre himself, thought she was marvellous and before the end of the war she was one of the heads of the broadcasting section. Her boss, Roger Ould, had been Basil Dean's casting director at Ealing Studios before the war. After the war he returned to his old job under Michael Balcon and, when he retired, nominated Margaret to succeed him. So one might say that her timely shout at Woolwich launched her on a successful career. But none of it would have happened if I hadn't have picked up Cynthia at the stage door of the King's Theatre, Glasgow, and if she hadn't have introduced me to Len Hunt in Oxford and if — and so on.

CHAPTER FOURTEEN

We returned to Oxford in filthy weather. It was a repeat of the previous year with Rugby and Soccer games being cancelled, Rowing disrupted and snow and slush barring the way to the bath house. To add to this initial misery I found to my shame that I had failed my Chaucer exam which I had taken at the end of the Michaelmas Term. If I had passed it I would have had a wartime degree which would have gladdened the hearts of my parents and no doubt would have enhanced such career prospects as I might have had. But the shame of it was that it was Chaucer, Nevill Coghill's favourite subject and one which any of his students would have been expected to sail through. So much for over-confidence. I was deeply disappointed but rationalised it by telling Nevill that I intended to come back after the war if I survived and do the thing properly.

Meanwhile domestic matters filled our time and attention. Jimmy Somner was elected JCR President with R.H. Martin as Secretary. John Boxshall, David Aiers and I seem to have been elected to the Committee. Derek Dawson was still Captain of Soccer, complaining loudly that the weather had restricted him to only two games. But the Senior Training Corps began to be increasingly demanding, probably because the beginning of 1942 marked a particularly low period for our fortunes in the war. Pearl Harbour may have forced the Americans in, but it was followed by the loss of Singapore, the sinking of the Repulse and the Prince of Wales, and severe set-backs in the desert. Obviously some-one in authority had decided that the fault lay in the general unfitness for combat of the Oxford undergraduate and so it was ordered that we should parade for Physical

The Front Quadrangle in winter. Photographed by Helen Martin, a Trinity undergraduate.

Training every Monday morning. This was reflected in College by a plea that dress regulations for breakfast in Hall should be relaxed. B. Quinan protested that it was farcical to have to dress properly for breakfast and then go back to one's room to change into sports clothes immediately after. However he was told firmly that Cadman would continue to enforce the dress rules but that he could wear an open neck shirt with a scarf, flannel trousers and a sports jacket for breakfast, so decorum was preserved and we had refused to allow the Hun or the STC to force us to change our rather stuffy ways.

Life in the College was also reflected in the entries in the suggestions book. D. Jones, having once again failed to get the Daily Herald, returned to the attack by recommending that we take the Soviet War News. Shoeten-Sack described it as "bloody dull" which roused the ire of T.E. Yeo who replied that "you can't call a paper bloody dull which records and illustrates the achievements of the only army in the world which has yet succeeded in pushing the Huns back and keeping them back." Shoeten-Sack defended his remark by saying that he wasn't criticising the Soviets but only the uninteresting way the stories were presented. "I object," he said, "to this political wrangling." Roger Hammick had the last word in this little fracas by protesting at "yet another Red paper in the JCR. Apart from one fighting for and one against there is very little difference between the Soviet and Nazi regimes." The use of the word `another' seems to indicate that perhaps Mr Jones had succeeded in breaching the staunchly conservative walls of the College before.

T.J.A. Kingan stirred up the sex war by asking "Do you think that something could be done about extending the time during which women are allowed into the College? Balliol, Wadham, and many other colleges allowed women to come into the college after seven. Is there any reason why Trinity cannot be trusted?" Martin, as JCR Secretary, replied that "in the summer, women are allowed in the College until 9 o'clock so I trust you will be satisfied next term." This deteriorated into

The Presidents Lodging where Tony Carson heard the cry of "Puss Puss"

a Trinity versus Balliol debate after David Van Zwannenberg had added, "And just look at Balliol and Wadham."

Tony Carson showed an interest in sanitation which may have been the first stirrings of a career which ended as Administrator of the Royal Perth Hospital in Western Australia. "Could something be done," he wrote, "about the revolting smell in the lats opposite the bath house?" Tony's letter about the President's black-out very accurately echoes the irritations of life without lights and also demonstrates the authentic voice of the undergraduate of 1942.

> "Sir, On entering the college tonight I observed a vast shaft of light pouring forth from the President's house. The door had not been left open by mistake for I soon discerned the magic words `puss-puss' being chanted into the night with praiseworthy regularity and patience. Might I suggest that before the President's cat is put out, the light might be extinguished in the President's hall? Not only so that the said cat should be allowed a little privacy but also so that there should be no risk of something being dropped on the College by a Jerry who might be simultaneously performing his nocturnal operations overhead?"

At the beginning of term the Conservative Association announced its programme with speeches by Lady Astor, Sir Roger Keyes, the Right honourable R.A. Butler, and Lord Vansittart, and a production of Sheridan's "The Critic". This was a continuation of their sponsorship of the Friends of the OUDS. They were also to debate the interesting motion, "That this house deplores the prospect of a woman Prime Minister."

To lighten our darkness somewhat, February saw the arrival of the Sadlers Wells Ballet with Margot Fonteyn and Robert Helpman. The orchestra conducted by Constant Lambert. This was, I think, the first chance we had of seeing Helpman's "Hamlet" ballet with his Nevill Coghill opening. His "Comus" received much acclaim although I thought that the sudden intrusion of the human voice, especially Helpman's rather fluting tones, reciting Milton was a distraction. The Rhythm Club continued to operate and Derek Dowdall and I contributed an article to the Cherwell called "What Is This Thing Called Jazz?" The fact that we had to try to explain it in such rudimentary terms shows how revolutionary we had been in starting a Jazz Club the year before.

Sitting one morning in Elliston's we were joined by Michael Flanders dressed as a sailor, looking incredibly handsome like someone out of the chorus of "Hit The Deck". He had just joined the Navy and had come to say his farewells. I think we were all convinced that we were in the presence of the future Laurence Olivier or successor to Gielgud. He had the looks, the talent and far more charm. He became another war casualty by contracting polio and the next time I saw him he was in a wheel chair. Although he bravely carved himself out a brilliant career there is no doubt that the stage was deprived of a mighty and never to be developed talent.

We were in the throes of plotting our production of "The Critic" which was due to open in the Taylorian on February 17th. I was also setting up for a production by the French Club which was to play there in the preceeding week. It was a good test for our Theatre Guild Co-Operative.

In the meantime, Glynne Wickham had thought of mounting a cabaret style show to raise funds and, for several evenings, the two of us could be seen rehearsing a Carmen Miranda number called "Minnie from Trinidad" with me drumming and Glynne dancing. That seems to be as far as we got.

"The Critic" was an entirely undergraduate affair with Nevill Coghill presiding paternalistically while Glynne drove us enthusiastically into what we knew would be our final fling. We did it in modern dress with a few interpolations such as Mr Dangle listening to a programme on his wireless called "Sweet, hot and black, a programme of coffee time music." Jack Becke changed from his suave front-of-house role to that of Mr Sneer and Rognwald Gunn played an ebullient Mr Puff. Trinity was well represented with Tony Carson, Byng Husband, George Wood and me. We were able to make a virtue out of the difficulties of staging a play in the Taylorian with special effects that didn't work, curtains that stuck and scenery that had to be hastily held up. As a merry romp it suited our mood because we realised that we would soon be separated and scattered throughout the forces.

In the Oxford Magazine, Leonard Rice-Oxley said that "the whole cast acted with gusto and discrimination", while the Oxford Mail, under the heading "Sheridan Modernised in Oxford - the Critic with plus fours and the Lambeth Walk" questioned whether

"the foppish elegance of Sheridan's whimsical and witty dandies, with their old world grace and affection, could ever be personified by a hale and hearty young man in plus fours, and the daintiness of Sheridan's brilliant lines should ever be merged with a gramophone record of 'The Lambeth Walk' is a debatable point." It went on, "In last night's production of 'The Critic' at the Taylorian, Oxford, given by the Friends of the Oxford University Dramatic Society, the players wore modern dress and determined efforts had been made to make references topical, although the bulk of the original script remained as a frame for the innovations which, while undoubtedly amusing, tended to make the style more commonplace. The fact that it was a first performance may have accounted for the somewhat ragged finish of the production, and although there were pauses, many of the principal actors were inclined to swallow their words or to speak them too quickly."

Under the sub-heading "Capable Acting" the Mail continued,

"Among the circle at Mr Dangle's house, Mr Sneer (Jack Becke) probably came as near to catching the mood of the author as any. He was agreeably languid, critical and superior.
The tempo was speedied up when Mr Puff presented his complicated tragedy. The burlesque was well caught, and a good performance was given by Roger Green as Tilburina, Tony Carson as Sir Christopher Hatton, and Byng Husband as Don Ferolo Whiskerandos.

The page of the Oxford Mail which placed a picture of a young sailor lost at sea in the middle of the write-up. In today's Radio the ENSA half-hour is at 8.30 on the Forces programme.

Nice studies of character were given among the minor parts by Richard Walheim (Interpreter), Robert Dudley (Lord Burleigh) and George Wood (Beefeater). Mr J.H. Nelson left doubt whether he was a member of the cast or not as he wandered unconcernedly and naturally about the stage. The play which runs to the end of this week is being produced by Mr Glynne Wickham."

That seemed to be a pretty fair summary of our efforts, but in fact it is true, to quote the Oxford Magazine, that "the whole performance owed much to Mr Glynne Wickham."

By a co-incidence the write-up appeared alongside the BBC programme advertising my sister's ENSA Half Hour. Unfortunately the column was also split rather inappropriately by a picture of a young sailor who had recently died at sea. Perhaps it was meant as an implied rebuke. In fact we all felt that, by our determination to carry on as normally as possible, we were showing a proper defiance. Many years later Glynne Wickham wrote,

"It was a time when the cultural amenities of Oxford life were just as severely rationed as were food and clothes. Most of us felt these productions moreover to be one of the big experiences of our lives, opening our minds in a way nothing else had done to Shakespeare's skill as a dramatist. Nevill Coghill was commonly regarded as one of the most stimulating teachers we had ever met. All my own thinking about plays and play production, even to the creation of a drama department in another University, has stemmed from this experience."

I have often wondered whether Nevill, in his modesty, ever realised the lasting influence he had on our lives and the affection we had for him.

My last theatrical activity was also a musical one. The University Musicians Club, under the chairmanship of Bruce Montgomery, had formed a rehearsal orchestra which I had joined as percussionist. David Cox was our initial conductor and then Sandy Faris took over to steer us through a performance of "H.M.S. Pinafore." "The Critic" had finished on the Saturday night and "Pinafore" opened on the following Tuesday the 24th, playing at 2.30 and 8 p.m. with another performance on Wednesday at 2.30, so my Theatre Guild crew must have worked like beavers over the week-end.

It was a pity that bookings for the hall only made it possible to do one evening performance. The Oxford Magazine commented that "with a real live undergraduate opera playing at the Taylorian from whose doors people were turned away, who will tell us that Oxford's spare-time activities have not stood up to the strains of war." Both the Magazine and The Cherwell were enthusiastic. "This sort of thing, to get across to-day, must rollick," said The Cherwell, "and the Musician's Club production did that in fine style. A good time was obviously being had by all, including the audience. The musical side of the production was extremely well dealt with, the orchestra, conducted by Sandy Faris, played perfectly con brio." The Oxford Magazine commented on Anthony Dearle's "excellent singing and facial acting" as Corcoran, and David Warwick's "authentically Savoyard dancing and gestures", although The Cherwell was less complimentary.

"The fault of the actors was chiefly that so few of them could act." Still everyone agreed that it was a "most enjoyable evening", and congratulated the producer, James Landon, on his successful combination of "theatrical and musical elements in so refreshing and naive an entertainment."

Paddy's friend Ursula Cartledge and a Mr Willner were given credit for "their charming scenery."

My own recollection of the evening performance was the shocked look on the face of a bearded Don in the audience, seated in the front row with his knees crushed beside my drummer's position in the crowded orchestra, when I accompanied David Warwick's "Savoyard dancing" with some distinctly off-beat rhythms of my own.

That was the end of my stint as Stage Manager of the Friends of the OUDS. I handed over that and the organisation of the Theatre Guild to my carrot starved friend in Magdalen and began the dreary business of packing. Glynne was off to the Air Force and we made a light-hearted pact to come back and carry on where we had left off. David Marsh, who remained my closest friend in the college after Paddy and David Humphreys went down, and I sat contemplatively for the last time listening to Deanna Durbin singing his favourite songs and wondering whether we would ever experience such contentment again. We remembered so many small episodes. The time David Aiers had shocked us by appearing in a pair of green corduroy trousers. Was it really because corduroy required three less clothing coupons than other clothing materials?

Was it he or David Humphreys who had dismissed the whole of womankind with a wave of the hand and the condemnatory, "After all what is woman but a couple of whatnots and a twat"? There had been so much love and laughter that it was difficult to believe that it was all over so soon. It was all over for Frank Margesson's father too as recorded in a last cheeky paragraph in the Cherwell.

"It is gratifying to notice the attention Mr Churchill seems to pay to the dicta of University politicians (bless their long furry ears)" wrote Flavus. "On Thursday last the Union decided that a cabinet reconstruction was necessary: on Friday it came. On Saturday the President of the Conservative Association declared war on the Conservative Central Office: on Sunday Margesson was driven from the War Office. It just shows, doesn't it."

I packed up my room for the last time. It was strange that my rather shabby suite had become such a home to me in so short a time. I left my brown bakelite wireless set and some bits and pieces of crockery and ash trays with North to stow away in his cupboard. They, with my scruffy commoner's gown, were my hostages to fortune.

Walking round saying my farewells I realised how generations of us had padded through these same precincts, making little impression but being ourselves impressed. Others would take over now. Nothing much would change. Firewatchers would still toss the occasional empty bottle into the Balliol garden and someone would be bound to make the college clock strike thirteen at midnight. A new generation would climb in over the St John's bicycle shed, bawdy songs would still be sung, and Cadman would continue to hold court and impose his disciplinary presence between the Buttery and the Hall.

Our luggage was piled up at the gate outside the Porter's lodge. Posters advertising the O.U. Rhythm Club and "The Critic" flapped in the breeze on the notice board under the Chapel arch. A last look back as the taxi took me to the station, past Elliston's and Taphouses and the New Theatre down George Street to the outer edge of town. And so farewell.

the Air Force and we made a light-hearted pact to come back and carry on where we had left off. David Marsh, who remained my closest friend in the college after Paddy and David Humphreys went down, and I sat contemplatively for the last time listening to Deanna Durbin singing his favourite songs and wondering whether we would ever experience such contentment again. We remembered so many small episodes. The time David Aiers had shocked us by appearing in a pair of green corduroy trousers. Was it really because corduroy required three less clothing coupons than other clothing materials?

Was it he or David Humphreys who had dismissed the whole of womankind with a wave of the hand and the condemnatory, "After all what is woman but a couple of whatnots and a twat"? There had been so much love and laughter that it was difficult to believe that it was all over so soon. It was all over for Frank Margesson's father too as recorded in a last cheeky paragraph in the Cherwell.

"It is gratifying to notice the attention Mr Churchill seems to pay to the dicta of University politicians (bless their long furry ears)" wrote Flavus. "On Thursday last the Union decided that a cabinet reconstruction was necessary: on Friday it came. On Saturday the President of the Conservative Association declared war on the Conservative Central Office: on Sunday Margesson was driven from the War Office. It just shows, doesn't it."

I packed up my room for the last time. It was strange that my rather shabby suite had become such a home to me in so short a time. I left my brown bakelite wireless set and some bits and pieces of crockery and ash trays with North to stow away in his cupboard. They, with my scruffy commoner's gown, were my hostages to fortune.

Walking round saying my farewells I realised how generations of us had padded through these same precincts, making little impression but being ourselves impressed. Others would take over now. Nothing much would change. Firewatchers would still toss the occasional empty bottle into the Balliol garden and someone would be bound to make the college clock strike thirteen at midnight. A new generation would climb in over the St John's bicycle shed, bawdy songs would still be sung, and Cadman would continue to hold court and impose his disciplinary presence between the Buttery and the Hall.

Our luggage was piled up at the gate outside the Porter's lodge. Posters advertising the O.U. Rhythm Club and "The Critic" flapped in the breeze on the notice board under the Chapel arch. A last look back as the taxi took me to the station, past Elliston's and Taphouses and the New Theatre down George Street to the outer edge of town. And so farewell.

POSTSCRIPT

If you are not sure that you will come out of a tunnel, the daylight is dazzling. It was 1947 and life was grimmer than it had been in wartime. Rationing was stricter and the Winter of 1946/47 was cruel. But we worked and played with all the vigour of ones reprieved. We had survived.

To add to the zest for life that pervaded the University after the war, we were joined by hundreds of eager ex-service undergraduates enjoying their first flush of civilian freedom and, with them, an influx of those we called the school-boy undergraduates. So we had among the old campaigners my former school friend Lindsay Anderson who joined with Penelope Houston to create the film magazine "Sequence", Ludovic Kennedy whose father had won the VC in the gallant action of the Rawalpindi who edited The Isis, Peter Wildeblood who enlivened the Cherwell and mixed happily with the young Ken Tynan, John Schlesinger and Tony Richardson. It was the era of Sandy Wilson and Donald Swann, Dennis Mathew and Timothy Bateson, Hugo Charteris, the Anthonys Greenwood and Wedgewood-Benn, Peter King, Anthony Besch, Guy de Moubray, Tony Schooling, Geoffrey Sharp, Penelope Peters, Heather Couper, Jennifer Ramage, Elizabeth Zaiman, Pat Hackwood, Derek and Peggy Holroyd, Jack Viner and, of course, Corinne Hunt.

In sport the University Rugby XV was stacked with internationals including the marvellous pairing of South Africa's Ossie Newton-Thompson with Martin Donnelly of New Zealand, Syd Newman at full back and Trinity's Van Ryneveld brothers. In rowing Trinity provided the Raikes brothers, Tony

Rowe and the University cox in ex-fighter pilot Faulkner. It was an exciting time to be savoured in memory. But what of the survivors?

Glynne Wickham returned to resume leadership of the OUDS and went on to become the distinguished founder of the Chair of Drama at Bristol University.

Nevil Macready had a brief brush with the BBC as an announcer on their European service and then set himself to more serious matters, rising eventually to a Directorship of the Mobil company. He succeeded to his father's baronetcy and, on retirement, was able to employ his love of racing by becoming the Chairman of the British Racing Authority and his artistic interests by being a distinguished member of the British Arts Council and a Director of the Victoria and Albert Museum.

David Humphreys survived being shot through the neck while serving as a subaltern with the Oxfordshire and Buckinghamshire Light Infantry in Normandy, was called to the Bar and spent three years as Judicial Advisor to the Government of Bahrain. Before that he had had a brush with politics as the prospective Conservative candidate for the parliamentary seat of West Ham. He still keeps in touch with Trinity and has close connections with the University of Kent. He firmly denies all knowledge of the Oxford Book of Dirty Ditties and is certain that it was Paddy Engelbach who took it all down and, indeed, away.

I have had the pleasure of meeting Derek Dawson and Peter Balmer at the occasional College reunion which I have managed to attend and I met Tony Carson in Perth, Western Australia when he became Administrator of the Royal Perth Hospital.

Derek Dowdall returned to revive the O.U. Rhythm Club but after he went down and joined Crosse and Blackwell I lost touch with him when I went overseas.

The kindly Nevill Coghill, who so influenced us, went on to continue to lead the University as senior member of the OUDS and the ETC and then achieved belated public fame when his adaptation of Chaucer's "Canterbury Tales" became a long-running West End musical.

Michael Meyer, having served in the R.A.F, remained a

man of letters and became what he described as a "kind of expert on the Scandinavian languages and wrote enormous biographies of Ibsen and Strindberg and translated thirty-six of their plays." His recollections of Oxford can be read in his memoirs "Not Prince Hamlet" published by Secker in 1989 and by OUP in paperback in 1990.

John Heath-Stubbs became completely blind at the age of sixty but in 1995 was still alive and active and living in Bayswater, London.

Roy Porter embraced the Church and became a Canon.

Among the others, Reginald Barr became a learned Judge, Eddie Stuart a noted surgeon and his long-suffering room-mate Philip Larkin, a famous poet. Roy Jenkins became Roy Jenkins.

Of the non-University cast, my sister Margaret remained with ENSA until the end of the war and then went to Ealing Studios where she succeeded Roger Ould as Casting Director. She was responsible for either discovering or advancing the careers of Audrey Hepburn, Dirk Bogarde, Peter Finch, Jack Warner, Virginia MacKenna and many others. Major productions which she cast included "The Cruel Sea" which re-established the war-interrupted career of Jack Hawkins and gave Donald Sinden his first starring role. She transferred briefly to the Rank Organisation when Ealing was sold and then became Casting Director in London for the J. Walter Thompson agency. She retired to look after our aging parents in the Isle of Mull.

My other sister Annabel's husband Terence Carothers was killed off Elba with the Royal Marines in 1944. She never remarried and eventually joined Margaret in retirement in the Isle of Mull to write her novel "Kilcaraig", published by Heineman shortly before her tragically early death from cancer.

Len Hunt developed his L.W. Hunt Drum Manufacturing company into a flourishing business which he sold in due course to retire to Eastbourne.

Cynthia Clifford had married by the time I returned from the Army and settled happily with her husband Stan Phillips in Wanstead. When I managed to contact her to borrow the photographs which appear in this book she was about to celebrate her Golden Wedding. Our photograph together,

John & Cynthia

snapped by a kindly waitress at the Cumberland Hotel almost brings this chronicle full circle.

As for me, I returned to take over my old role of Stage Manager of the OUDS for a production of "The Pretenders" but got pneumonia helping Audrey Dunlop to build and paint the set and so missed being a part of University theatrical history. Later I did "Agamemnon" for the ETC which Glynne directed, played the drums with the Bandits for a couple of Commem Balls at Worcester and St John's and teamed with Denis Mathew and Donald Swann to provide the music for the ETC revues which helped to set Sandy Wilson on his way to fame. I spent a lot of time on the river helping to coach the rowers in that triumphant year when Trinity stayed Head of the River with one of the best Eights in its history. Fortunately I filmed it and the videotape is in the College archive. I now live in Perth,

Western Australia, having retired from a long stint as a presenter on radio and TV for the Australian Broadcasting Commission.

In 1994 I returned to Oxford to look for photographs and check on some facts and figures. Superficially it was much the same although many of the colleges have sprouted some hideous and inappropriate residential appendages. Trinity's contribution to this is an attachment to the College library of a staircase of almost mediaeval inaccessibility overlooking the garden, but this has been compensated for by a well designed and sympathetic addition which stands where our bath-house used to be.

Of course all the Colleges are now co-educational or unisex or whatever the current expression may be. It was suggested to me that this had cut down the amount of male rowdyism which used to take place but Phil Landon must be turning in his grave. David Humphreys took the view that experience was better than dirty ditties. Certainly the easy and open atmosphere which existed in 1941 no longer applies. Trinity, and presumably all the other colleges, has succumbed to the siege mentality of the nineties and is beset with locks and coded buttons and dire warnings against thieves and intruders on every staircase. As a contribution to civilised living, the lavatories and bathrooms which male and female students seem to share are papered with exhortations to the girls to dispose of their tampons in a manner that will not cause offence or embarrassment to their confreres.

The College garden is still beautiful but the famous Lime Walk is no more, having succumbed to either old age or disease. The great gate from the garden onto Parks Road remains welded shut, awaiting the restoration of the Stuarts, in spite of Hanoverian denials. The College hall has been tarted up to look like a film set of a college hall which indeed it became on one occasion, but the old buildings still retain their friendly dignity.

My room above the Hall, number 13, staircase 11, has, like so much of the world, been subdivided and what was my sitting-room has become a bed-sitter with hot and cold running water and the old fireplace boarded up. My former bedroom has been similarly treated and is now number 14. David Marsh's and Paddy Engelbach's rooms have suffered the same fate.

The static water tank and its rose garden outside the Library has given way to a paved courtyard which, I was told, is the roof of the Norrington Room of Blackwell's bookshop next door which has burrowed under the college.

All the pubs seem to have survived but not the famous shove ha'penny boards which have not only disappeared but caused some puzzlement when I enquired about them. Those two places that were so much the centre of our lives, Elliston's and Taphouses, have disappeared although the buildings still remain as part of Debenham's. In a world of self-service and plastic there are no neat waitresses to serve on you any more. Where Fuller's dispensed their delightful walnut cake you will find the Burger King and the Beehive has become The Nosebag. Happily the Taj Mahal has survived where it was but further down the Turl the barber's shop is now but a sign.

Of the theatres and cinemas, the Playhouse continues but the New Theatre is now the Apollo. The Ritz became the Cannon but is now another MGM as is the old Super in Magdalen Street. The Electra was pulled down to become Marks & Spencers. The Scala in Walton Road is now the Phoenix, the Regal Cowley a bingo hall and the New in Headington had been demolished. But the essential Oxford still survives as it has always done even through the vandalism and iconoclasm of the most disastrous century in human history and will, I trust, always remain an oasis of calm and civilised existence.

Many of the players in this brief chronicle have died but there are some to whom this book is specially dedicated. Of those who matriculated with me in 1940, David Marsh was killed in France after D-Day, Vernon St John was shot down in the RAF and Paddy Engelbach, having survived being shot down and imprisoned as a night fighter pilot, stayed on in the RAF, married Kim Philby's sister and was killed a few years later when the plane he was flying hit a hill. M.E. Lock, C.D. Oliphant, E.G.A. Sotheron-Estcourt and Roger Hammick were also killed. Altogether one hundred and thirty two Trinity men died for their country in World War Two.

Of those happy thespians of our productions of "Othello", "Much Ado", "Hamlet" and "The Critic", Hallam Fordham,

Bryan Henshaw, John Goldingham, and Rognwald Gunn did not survive.

In writing this memoir I hope that I have been able to recreate a little of the spirit and atmosphere of the times through which we lived so that "the memory be green."

The sign is there but not the shop where they had "The astringent that made you think they had shrunk your head." –The Turl, 1994

The Gloucester Arms behind the Playhouse.

Where the STC paraded, only the crunch of Tourist's feet echo against the walls of Christchurch College –The Broadwalk 1994

The Welsh Pony at Gloucester Green

The Lamb and Flag. Still with us in 1994.

Fuller's Teashop is now the Burger King.

This was Taphouse's Music Shop where the sounds of the Bandit's rehearsals used to be heard emanating from the rehearsal room on the first floor.

The Beehive is now the Nosebag.

The Taj Mahal Restaurant is still on the first floor of the corner building in the Turl.

This used to be Elliston & Cavell. The famous Tea room was on the first floor below the two far flags.

The Electra Cinema is now Marks & Spencer's in Queen's Street.

This used to be the Super Cinema where the cry of "Well rowed, Balliol" started a pre-war riot.

The New Theatre has become The Apollo.

The back alley that led to the "rears" & bath-house. The bush on the right marks the old entrance —"you'll need a torch, sir."

The remains of the old bath-house building abuts the new student accomodation.

INDEX

A

Abrahams, I.J.   116
Agate, James   1, 23, 67, 74, 172
Aiers, David P.   15, 91, 103, 145, 170, 196, 205
Aldrich, Ronnie   163
Alexander, Terence   154
Allen, George   184
Ambrose   124
Anderson, Lindsay   207
Anderson, N.   171
Andrew, David   144
Arden, Bob   162
Arden, Doreen   153
Armstrong   167
Ashcroft, M.A.   141
Ashcroft, Peggy   79
Ashmore, Peter   22
Asquith, Anthony   121
Astor, Lady   199
Attlee, Clement   57

B

Bacon, Max   163, 176
Baddeley, Angela   22
Bahadoorsingh, I.J.   141
Balcon, Michael   195
Baldwin, Stanley   104
Balmer, Peter   83, 116, 145, 208
Banks, Leslie   23
Barker, Harry   154
Barr, Reginald   16, 18, 32, 42, 43, 60, 62, 79, 82, 85, 91, 96, 110, 114, 117, 125, 209
Barriteau, Carl   176, 192
Bateson, Timothy   207
Bayley, Peter   115
Bayliss, Bill   14
Beachcomber   172
Becke, Jack   182, 184, 200, 201

Belfrage, Bruce   125
Bennison, Geoffrey   111
Berners, Lord   180, 184, 186
Besch, Anthony   207
Bibby, Derek   106, 145, 167
Bird, H.   141
Blackford, Alec   119
Blake, Cyril   177
Blake, Martin   59, 60
Bogarde, Dirk   209
Bolton, S.   14, 30, 33, 146, 168, 169
Bond   30
Booth, Webster   124
Boothby, John   81
Bowden, Margaret   144, 184
Boxshall, John   145
Bradley, Josephine   124
Bretherton, Freddie   162
Bright, Gerald   157
Brinson, Derek   113, 114, 115
Bromley, Tommy   192
Brothers, Deniz   192
Brown, Ivor   76, 172
Brown, Pamela   22, 74, 75, 76
Brown, Rosemary   188
Browne, Sam   162
Bryson, John   182
Buchanan, Jack   139, 153
Budd, Harry   150, 154
Burke, Patricia   139
Butler, J.   171
Butler, Rt Hon R.A.   140, 141, 199
Buttrum, Ann   144
Byrde, C.G.   32
Byron, John   22, 74, 76

C

Cadman   28, 29, 36, 37, 138, 197, 206
Camber, Len   195

223

Campbell, Sir Colin   26
Campbell, Willie   71
Campbell-Colquhoun   30
Carless, Dorothy   195
Carothers, Annabel   36, 59, 63, 64, 68, 70, 91, 209
Carothers, Fionna   63, 64
Carothers, Terence   209
Carson, Tony   145, 198, 199, 200, 201, 208
Carter-Mather, Bud   118, 119
Cartledge, Ursula   128, 204
Carton-Kelly, L.D.   14, 30, 145
Cassandra   172
Caste, Renna   91, 153
Charteris, Hugo   207
Churchill, Randolph   57
Claes, Johnny   163, 175, 176
Clapham and Dwyer   124
Clapperton, Jock   131, 132
Clare, Mary   139
Clarke, L.   141
Clifford, Cynthia   67, 68, 72, 73, 91, 92, 93, 94, 122, 123, 153, 156, 157, 161, 189, 194, 195, 209, 210
Coghill, Nevill   15, 17, 19, 23, 52, 54, 56, 62, 116, 146, 179, 182, 184, 196, 199, 200, 203, 208
Cole, G.D.H.   15
Colin, Sid   163
Colson   9, 10, 28
Comyn, J.G.   141
Cooper, Jack   163
Copley, Peter   22
Cornwell, Brian   49
Cornwell, Roger   49
Cotton, Billy   124
Couper, Heather   207
Courtneidge, Cicely   63, 72, 79, 91, 94, 95, 122, 150, 153, 156
Coverdale, J.M.   143
Cox, David   203
Crowther, Eunice   94, 153
Crutchley, Rosalie   23, 74
Cummings, Jock   162, 163

Cunningham-Craig, John   188
Currie, Peter   145
Curtis, M.R.   15, 28, 30

D

d'Albie, Julian   22, 74
Daniels, Bebe   125
Dare, Zena   144
Darlington, Jim H.   14, 137, 138
Davenport   28
Davies, Duncan   8, 168, 169
Davies, Gordon   60, 125, 140
Davison, David   188
Dawson, Derek   14, 30, 145, 167, 168, 169, 171, 196, 208
Day-Lewis, Cecil   22
de Balliol, John   25
de Hamil, Ian   97, 144
de Moubray, Guy   207
Dean, Basil   195
Deans, Danny   177
Dearle, Anthony   204
Decima, Mickie   153
Desmond, Florence   124, 194
Dixon   80, 177
Dixon, Frank   80, 177
Dixon, M.F.   14
Dobson, Quentin   184
Dodd, Pat   163
Donnelly, Martin   207
Doughty   154
Douglas, J.A.T.   141
Dowdall, Derek   57, 172, 173, 199, 208
Doyle, Bunny   194
Drayton, Alfred   79
Drury, R.A.B.   8, 14, 30
Du Santoy   28
Dudley, Robert   203
Dunlop, Audrey   210

E

Edwards, Jimmy   92
Eley, John   184

Elliot, Bill   173, 175, 176
Elliston   35, 43, 55, 125, 173, 200, 206, 212, 219
Elrick, George   64, 176
Engelbach, Paddy   8, 14, 25, 28, 30, 36, 53, 79, 83, 85, 95, 97, 103, 116, 123, 132, 145, 208, 211, 212
Evans, Betty   140
Evans, George   162
Evans, J.   8, 28, 30
Evans, Winifred   22
Eyre, A.G.   14
Eyre, John   60, 113, 115

F

Faris, Sandy   203, 204
Farrer, Austin   21, 38
Faulkner   208
Featherstonehaugh, Buddy   176
Feldman, Monty   163
Feldman, Robert   163
Feldman, Victor   163
Fenhoulet, Paul   163
Fierstone, George   177
Finch, Peter   209
Fitzmaurice, Lord   85
Flanagan and Allen   124
Flanders, Michael   60, 79, 115, 140, 143, 145, 188, 200
Fletcher, Cyril   40
Fleure, J.L.   143
Flint, P.   171
Fonteyn, Margot   199
Foot, Michael   140, 141
Fordham, Hallam   79, 184, 212
Frankau, Ronald   124
Frazer, Simon   188
Frisby, Roger   81

G

Garibian, S.A.   116
Geraldo   124, 154, 157, 162, 163, 176, 194, 195
Gibbons, Grinling   19

Gielgud, John   60, 115, 144
Giles   172
Gillie, Jean   153, 154
Gilmour, Sally   145
Gold, Harry   192
Goldingham, John   144, 184, 213
Gollanz, Victor   58
Gordon, G.S.   141
Gordon, Sabina   153
Gore, Walter   145
Grapelly, Stephane   192
Gray   167
Gray, R.   141
Green, Laurence   91, 122, 148, 150, 151, 152, 153, 156
Green, Roger   184, 201
Greenwood, Anthony   207
Grey, Beryl   117
Groves, Olive   163
Gunn, Rognwald   184, 200, 213
Gurney   30
Gynes   34, 35

H

Hackwood, Pat   207
Halama, Alicja   140
Hale, Binnie   139
Hall, Henry   124, 177
Hall, Mary   184
Hammick, Roger   168, 169, 171, 198, 212
Handley, Tommy   124
Hare, Robertson   79
Harper-Nelson, John   22, 119, 137, 184, 203
Harper-Nelson, Margaret   3
Harris, Robert   181
Harrison, Rex   79
Hauser, Frank   140
Hawkins, Jack   209
Hayward, Susan   120
Hazell, Hy   153
Heath-Stubbs, John   79, 209
Hedges, Lionel   44

Helpman, Robert   182, 199
Henderson, Chick   162
Henshaw, Bryan   184, 213
Henson, Leslie   139
Hepburn, Audrey   209
Herbert, A.P.   96
Hersch, G.   141
Hibbert, Stuart   125
Hickey, William   172
Higham, Thomas   15, 38
Hill, Anthony   184
Hill, Benny   92
Hinton, Antony   79
Hodgens   32, 33, 102, 145
Hodgson   167
Hodgson, Maurice   175
Hollingworth, Clare   59
Holloway, Stanley   139
Holroyd, Derek and Peggy   207
Hope-Nicholson, Felix   98
Hopkins, Clare   1
Hopkinson, N.J.   169
Houston, Penelope   207
Howard, Leslie   121
Howe, George   144
Howerd, Frankie   92
Hulbert, Claude   94, 95, 153, 156
Hulbert, Jack   63, 72, 79, 91, 94, 146, 149, 150, 152, 153, 156, 191
Hulbert, Pamela-Rosemary   94, 154
Humphreys, David C.   91, 95, 103, 137, 138, 145, 205, 208, 211
Hunt, Corinne   207
Hunt, Len   93, 118, 154, 157, 162, 192, 195, 209
Hunter, Jackie   195
Hurdis-Jones, Freddie   79
Husband, Byng   145, 167, 180, 184, 200, 201
Hutchinson, Leslie 'Jiver'   22, 107, 124, 192
Hyde, John   5
Hylton, Jack   119

I

Ireland, Anthony   22

J

Jackson, Edgar   176
Jacobsen, Jock   163
James, Gola   153
Jeans, Ursula   144
Jenkins, Claude   141
Jenkins, Roy H.   56, 141, 209
Jenkins, Tim   192
Jerrold, Mary   139, 144
Johnson, Amy   121
Johnson, Ken   163, 177
Jones, D.G.B.   171, 197
Jones, K.G.I.   141

K

Katz, Dick   177
Kaye   14, 30
Kennedy, Ludovic   207
Kennedy, Rosamund   111, 113
Kerr, Deborah   76
Keyes, Sidney   79, 109
Kinchin-Smith, M.   141
King, Nosmo   124
King, Peter   207
Kingan, T.   171, 198
Kirkwood, Pat   195
Kitchen, Fred Junior   153, 154
Knox, Collie   172
Konarski, Cjeslaw   140

L

Lambert, Constant   199
Lambert, Julie-Ann   1
Landauer, Spud   44
Landon, James   184
Landon, Philip   28, 38, 170
Landstad, Sigrid   22
Lane, Lupino   22
Larkin, Philip   80, 96, 109, 209
Laski   58

Law, Richard   141
Laye, Evelyn   161, 194
Layton, Turner   124
Lazarus, Alan   81, 177
Lee, Benny   163
Lejeune, Carol   172
Leon, Jack   193
Levens, Professor   173
Liddell, Alvar   125
Lipton, Celia   192
Lipton, Syd   192
Livesey, Roger   76, 144
Lock, E.M.   8, 10, 14, 30, 168
Lock, M.E.   14, 30, 168, 170, 171, 212
Loss, Joe   124, 162
Lundy, Doreen   162
Lyon, Ben   125

M

MacDonnell, A.G.   23, 74
MacFadyen, Chrissie   70
MacInnes, Neil   70
MacKenzie, Pamela   127, 146
Maclagan, Michael   38
MacLeod, Joseph   125
MacPherson, A.G.   18, 19, 30, 32, 61, 85, 117
Macready, Nevil   47, 48, 89, 109, 123, 125, 145, 148, 173, 191
Maden, Arthur   163
Magee, E.L.   14, 30
Margesson, Frank   15, 58, 145, 205
Mark, Alison   184
Marsh, David H.   8, 14, 25, 28, 30, 85, 89, 91, 103, 145, 147, 163, 167, 205, 211, 212
Marsh, Roy   163
Martin, Betty   94, 153
Martin, R.H.   28, 196
Mathew, Denis   81, 210
Mathew, Nigel   14, 83, 103, 116, 145, 170, 207

McCallum, R.B.   141
McQuater, Tommy   162
Menuhin, Yehudi   110
Meyer, Michael   21, 22, 58, 78, 115, 144, 208
Midgeley, Bobby   176
Miller, David   162, 163, 176
Miller, Max   124
Milligan, Spike   92
Moffat, John   23
Mollison, Ian M.   14, 96, 138, 145
Monte, Lionel   154
Montgomery, Bruce   203
Moody, Wally   176
Morgan, Charles   16
Morphett, Derek   35, 60, 115, 125
Morven, Myrette   153
Moss   30, 158
Murray   28

N

Nares, Owen   79
Neagle, Anna   122
Needham, Peter   176
Neville, Derek   176
Newman, Syd   207
Newton-Thompson, Ossie   207
Nicholson, Nora   22
Niven, David   121
Noel-Baker, Philip   59
North   5, 6

O

O'Connor, Cavan   124
Oliphant, C.D.   14, 137, 138, 212
Oliver, Vic   124, 125
Osborne   44
Ould, Roger   157, 195, 209
Owen, Reg   177

P

Pakenham-Walsh, Bill   170, 171
Pallis, Christopher   184

Palliser, Michael   188
Palmer, Lilli   79
Parker   14, 30
Parker, Brian   175
Parker, Duggie   44
Parker, Stanley   20, 21, 117
Parrington   167
Parry, Harry   124, 163, 176
Partridge, Simon   8, 28, 30, 32, 100, 168, 171
Pavlow, Muriel   98, 144
Peters, Penelope   207
Peters, Ray   36, 103, 145, 169
Philby, Kim   212
Phillips, Stan   209
Pilkington, C.L.   14
Pinsent, John   144
Pogson, E.O. "Eddie"   119
Pomfret, Nickie   180, 184
Pope, Sir Thomas   25
Pope, W. MacQueen   193
Porter, Roy   80, 188, 209
Potter, Gillie   124
Powell, Dilys   172
Probst, Bob   93, 154, 156
Profumo   154
Pughe, George   122, 149, 153

Q

Quartermaine, Leon   144
Quinan, B.   197
Quinlan, J.B.P.   171

R

Raikes brothers   207
Ramage, Jennifer   207
Rampton, Jack   14, 28, 117
Randolph, Elsie   139
Rawlings, Margaret   16, 59, 116, 144
Reid, Jock   163
Reinhold, D.L.   14, 28, 168
Rice-Oxley   30
Rice-Oxley, Leonard   201

Richardson, Tony   207
Riddle, Kenneth   141
Ritchard, Cyril   139
Robertson   167
Robinson, Vandeleur   59
Roger, Sir Keyes   199
Ros, Edmundo   163
Ross   44
Rowe, Tony   207
Roy, Derek   92
Roy, Harry   124

S

Sargent, Malcolm   158
Schlesinger, John   207
Schooling, Tony   207
Scott, C.P.   23
Scott, Rosemary   22
Scrymgeour-Wedderburn, David   130, 137
Seal, Esmund   96, 119
Sellers, Peter   92
Sharp, Geoffrey   207
Shaw, Bert   177
Shearing, George   124, 163, 176, 177, 192
Shepherd, Pamela   153
Shoeten-Sack, E.L.N.   14, 30, 167, 170, 197, 198
Simple, Peter   172
Sinden, Donald   209
Slingsby   44
Smedley, John   40, 41
Smith, Esmond   184
Smith, R.G.   30
Snell, C.V.I.   33
Somner, Jimmy   10, 14, 145, 168, 169, 171, 196
Sonin, Ray   176
Sotheron-Estcourt, E.G.A.   15, 212
South, Sonia   184
Spencer, Molly   79
St John, Vernon   8, 14, 28, 30, 32, 47, 48, 50, 52, 53, 85, 95, 98, 99,

100, 103, 109, 145, 206, 212
Stamp, Max   15
Staveley, M.S.   14, 30
Stenfalt, Norman   176
Stephens   30
Stetson   37
Stewart, Eddie   96
Stirling, Edward   59, 60, 62
Stirling, Monica   16, 59
Stirling, Pamela   59
Stobbs, J.   141
Stone, Christopher   107, 162, 176
Stone, Lew   124
Storey, R.G.   30
Straghan, E.   8
Strauss, George   58
Stuart, Eddie   209
Swann, Donald   81, 207, 210
Swinburne, Nora   144
Swing, Raymond Gram   125
Sylvester, Jimmy   176, 177
Sylvester, Victor   124, 176

T

Talbot-Harvey, Henry   184
Tann, Eric   163
Taphouse's music shop   35, 48, 55, 80, 173, 206, 212, 217
Tapsfield   44
Tauber, Richard   139
Taylor, A.R.   28, 35
Taylor, Basil   80
Taylor, R.A.   117
Telling, A.E.   141
Tempest, Marie   144
Temple-Carrington, A.G.   15
Thomas, J.G.   32
Thompson, Art   177
Thompson, Henry   94, 153
Thompson, R.R.   171
Tottenham, Benny   184
Toyne, Gabriel   16
Traill, Sinclair   173, 175
Tregarthen, Jeanette   114, 115

Trevor, Enid   153
Trower, Philip   144, 180, 184
Tully, Iris   91, 94, 153
Tynan, Kenneth P.   178, 207

V

Van Damm, Vivian   92
Van Ryneveld   207
Van Zwannenberg, David   15, 30, 145, 169, 171, 199
Vansittart, Lord   199
Vaughan, Hilda   59
Vickers, Michael   144
Villiers, Doreen   163, 195
Viner, Jack   207

W

Wade   30
Wakefield, Oliver   22, 124
Walbrook, Anton   157
Walheim, Richard   203
Ward, Ronald   144
Ward-Perkins, Bryan   1
Warner, E.C.H.   143
Warner, Jack   124, 209
Warwick, David   180, 184, 204
Waterhouse, Colonel   96
Waterstone, V.C.   116
Watson, Peggy   153
Waugh, W.A.O'N.   137, 138
Weaver, J.R.H.   31, 32, 38
Webb, Basil   94, 95
Wedgewood-Benn   207
Weir, Frank   176
Whiteman, Leonard   59
Wickham, Glynne   16, 24, 144, 179, 182, 183, 184, 187, 200, 203, 208
Wilcox, Herbert   121
Wildeblood, Peter   207
Wilkinson, Clive   10, 28, 30
Wilkinson, Ellen   58
Wilkinson, Ronnie   80
Williams, Emlyn   22

229

Williams, M.R.   14
Williams, Stephen   193
Willner   129, 204
Wilson, Harold   104, 178
Wilson, Sandy   207, 210
Winnick, Maurice   124
Winstone, Eric   124, 176
Wood, George   200, 203
Wood, Pat   59
Woodruff, Anthony   23
Wyndham-Lewis, Angela   22
Wynyard, Diana   79

Y

Yeldham-Taylor, Diana   80, 144, 184, 186
Yeo, T.E.   197
Young, Arthur   163
Young, John   175

Z

Zaiman, Elizabeth   207
Ziegler, Anne   124